All Buttoned Up

All Buttoned Up

12 Quilts from the Button Box

Loraine Manwaring and Susan Nelsen

 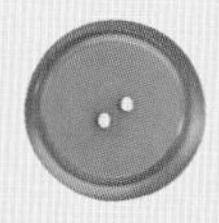 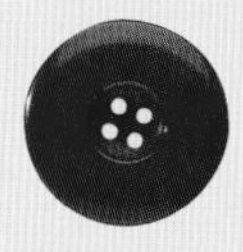  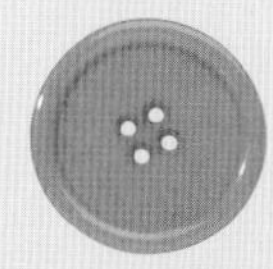 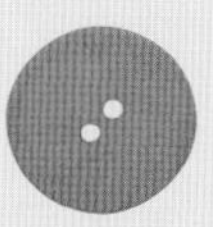   

That Patchwork Place® is an imprint of Martingale & Company®.

Martingale & Company
20205 144th Avenue NE
Woodinville, WA 98072-8478 USA
www.martingale-pub.com

Printed in China
11 10 09 08 07 06   8 7 6 5 4 3 2 1

Library of Congress Cataloging-in-Publication Data
Library of Congress Control Number: 2006020420

ISBN-13: 978-1-56477-706-5
ISBN-10: 1-56477-706-5

Mission Statement

Dedicated to providing quality products and service to inspire creativity.

Credits

President • Nancy J. Martin
CEO • Daniel J. Martin
COO • Tom Wierzbicki
Publisher • Jane Hamada
Editorial Director • Mary V. Green
Managing Editor • Tina Cook
Technical Editor • Laurie Baker
Copy Editor • Liz McGehee
Design Director • Stan Green
Illustrator • Laurel Strand
Cover and Text Designer • Regina Girard
Photographer • Brent Kane

Dedication

To our grandmother, Sophia Lucille Snyder Anderson.
Thank you for sharing your button box.

Acknowledgments

With thanks and great appreciation to:

Our families, for their patience and support;

Pam Mostek, for her encouragement and prodding;

United Notions, for wonderful buttons and trim;

JHB International, for buttons that inspire.

Contents

Opening Our Button Box

If you're a quilter, then you're most likely a collector. Many of us have a collection of fabrics, a collection of patterns, a collection of books, and more than likely, a collection of buttons.

The first button collection we knew about belonged to our grandmother. We played with her button box whenever we visited. The box was heavy as we lifted it down from its place in her sewing cupboard. It rattled and thumped with the sounds of hundreds of buttons shifting, a distinct sound that brought treasure to mind. We made piles of blue buttons, red buttons, yellow buttons, all colors of buttons. The buttons were cool to the touch as we ran our fingers through the cache in the box.

Today we have our own button boxes filled with some of those very buttons, as well as buttons we've accumulated in the years since we played together in our grandmother's closet. Various buttons accompanied us to Brownie Scouts or outside to play. Others are bits of family history, tied to people and events of importance to us. Years later, we find buttons that remind us of our own children—a button from a daughter's wedding dress or a son's first suit. Other buttons are there simply because we like them, and because neither of us can resist a novel or elegant button. We justify our willingness to buy buttons on a whim because we know that one of these days, we'll have a need for that perfect button.

Buttons are like candy to quilters. They whet our appetite for treats, and we add them to quilting-supply pantries already filled with fabric, patterns, and buttons. Buttons are easy to store in our sewing closets. No matter how many we have, there's always room for another!

What can we do with all of these buttons? This collection of quilts shows you what we've done with some of the buttons from our button boxes. Each quilt is embellished with buttons and is designed around our childhood recollections. In the "Button Box" that accompanies each project, you'll find information about the buttons and what inspired us to use them. Maybe some of our thoughts will strike familiar chords with you, and you'll remember similar events and times.

We hope our projects capture your interest and inspire you to get out your button boxes and put your buttons into action. Thanks for letting us share these button quilts with you.

—Loraine and Susan

What's in Your Button Box?

It's time to open your button box and see what you have. Chances are you'll find buttons that are quite old, as well as some that are very new. You may find that some buttons in your box have historical value and that many have sentimental value. Think of buttons as little pieces of art or as bits of personal or family history.

Buttons have been made from metal, leather, fabric, glass, pearl, shell, ceramic, bone, ivory, and even rubber! If you have vintage buttons, they might be made of early plastics like Bakelite or celluloid. Jet, which is anthracite coal, is another common material from which antique buttons were made.

Buttons have been used since prehistoric times—and not just for fashion. They've long been used for trading. In earlier times, trading buttons was a pastime popular with young boys. They gave the buttons names that indicated their characteristics. For example, "bangers" were large, flat, metal buttons used in place of pennies in pitching games. "Sinkeys" or "one-ers" were concave metal buttons with holes in them for sewing. "Shankeys" were either "two-ers" or "three-ers," depending on their size or rarity. "Liveries" were buttons from the uniforms of family servants and featured the family crest on them.

Young girls also collected buttons, threading them on strings to create charm strings, which were also known as memory strings. The first button on the string was known as a "touch" button, and then subsequent buttons were added to the string behind this button. Two rules applied to the charm string: no two buttons could be alike, and the buttons had to be gifts from family or friends. The buttons could be traded with friends, but the collector couldn't purchase the buttons.

The idea of a charm string was to collect a thousand unique and beautiful buttons. A button was highly prized if it had a story to go with it. For example, a young girl could share a story that a particular button was sewn on her great-grandmother's wedding gown, and so on. The more elaborate the button story, the more valuable the button.

Folklore has it that the collector needed 999 buttons and then, when the collector found her last button, she would meet her prince. Some stories claim that the last button would actually come from Prince Charming's coat. Most charm strings were never completed, and many were taken apart at a later time. However, some were wrapped in tissue and carefully tucked away. Today, intact Victorian charm strings are highly collectible.

Interestingly enough, charm strings have a connection to quilting. It's said that the collection of enough fabric squares to make a quilt with no fabric repetitions was influenced by this practice, and the quilts were called—you guessed it—Charm quilts.

Buttons, buttons everywhere!

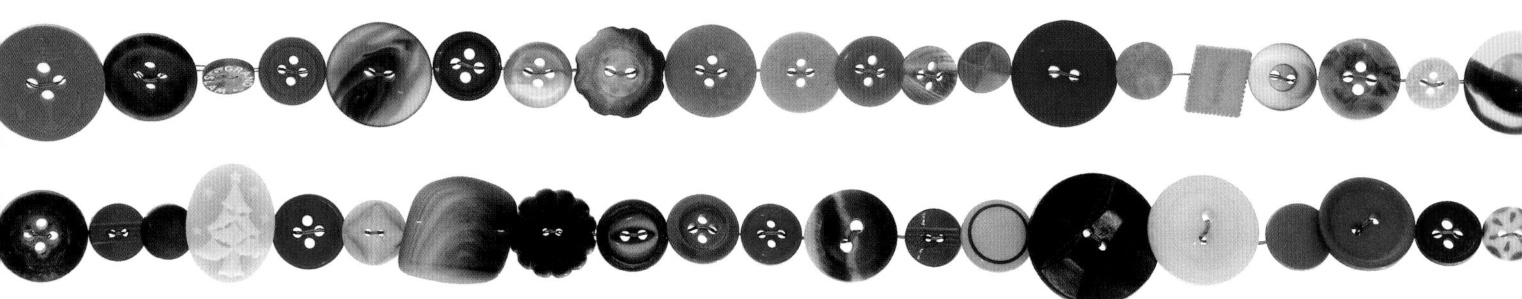

Charm strings

Begin now to add to your collection of buttons. Buttons are everywhere—maybe in a box, a junk drawer, or a jar. Search through your buttons one by one to see what memories they trigger. Discover what thoughts you have about an individual button. Look for an old family button box used by your mother or grandmother.

Check out antique stores, flea markets, and thrift stores for bags, jars, or boxes of buttons. Go through the old clothes at these shops and look for unusual buttons. Before you discard clothing, check for interesting buttons or ones that might have sentimental value.

Of course, brand-new buttons are fascinating and inspiring, too. Brilliant colors, unique shapes, and favorite themes might inspire a project built around particular buttons. Check out buttons at your local fabric store and go online to discover a fascinating world of buttons.

Tips for Attaching Buttons

Buttons generally come in two varieties. A shank button has a loop on the back for securing the button to the garment. A sew-through button has two or four holes through the surface for sewing the button to the garment.

You can use your sewing machine to apply sew-through buttons if your machine is equipped with a zigzag stitch and you can lower the feed dogs. This will save you time and ensure that the buttons are securely attached. Use a glue stick to tack each button to the quilt before you sew. Lower the feed dogs and set your machine for a zigzag stitch, with a stitch length wide enough to sew from one hole to the other. If the spacing is incorrect, it's easy to break a button or a needle.

On our first few projects, we hand sewed the buttons using all-purpose thread. But after stitching on so many, many buttons, we decided that tying buttons on with embroidery floss was the way to go when numerous buttons were required. We use a needle with a large eye to accommodate all six strands of floss, then we take a stitch through the holes of the button, leaving thread tails on the back of the quilt. The ends are then tied in a square knot and trimmed.

Attach buttons to the projects after all the quilting has been completed, and don't worry that there is quilting around the area where the buttons will be placed. The quilting won't interfere with the buttons.

Grandmother's Purses

Skill level: *Confident beginner*

Finished quilt: 34½" x 34½" • **Finished block:** 10" x 10"

All the purses in this quilt were inspired by a single button—saved from a coat belonging to my great-grandmother, Annie Duckworth Snyder. Though faded and well worn, it seemed the perfect button. I put it on the upper-left purse in this wall quilt.
—Loraine

Button Box

Buttons lend themselves perfectly to these purses, as embellishments and clasps. Some of the buttons have been in my button box for years, and others were purchased with a certain purse in mind.

Materials

Yardages are based on 42"-wide fabric unless otherwise noted.

⅜ yard *each* of 5 coordinating prints for appliqués
⅔ yard of pink dot print for block backgrounds
½ yard of white-and-black print for inner border
⅜ yard of black print for outer border
⅓ yard of black striped print for sashing
⅛ yard of paisley print for inner-border cornerstones
⅛ yard of black-and-rose check for sashing cornerstones
½ yard of black-and-pink floral print for binding
1⅛ yards of fabric for backing
40" x 40" piece of batting
1⅓ yards of 17"-wide paper-backed fusible web
6" of beaded trim for purse B
1 button, 1⅛" diameter, for purse A
1 button, ⅞" diameter, for purse B
4 buttons, ½" diameter, for purse C
1 button, 1⅜" diameter, for purse D
4 buttons, 1⅛" diameter, for inner-border cornerstones

Cutting

All measurements include ¼"-wide seam allowances.

From the pink dot print, cut:

- 2 strips, 10½" x 42"; crosscut into 4 squares, 10½" x 10½"

From the black striped print, cut:

- 4 strips, 2" x 42"; crosscut into 12 pieces, 2" x 10½"

From the black-and-rose check, cut:

- 1 strip, 2" x 42"; crosscut into 9 squares, 2" x 2"

From the white-and-black print, cut:

- 4 pieces, 3¼" x 25"

From the paisley print, cut:

- 1 strip, 3¼" x 42"; crosscut into 4 squares, 3¼" x 3¼"

From the black print, cut:

- 4 strips, 2½" x 42"

From the black-and-pink floral print, cut:

- 4 strips, 2¾" x 42"

Making the Blocks

1. Refer to "Appliquéing with Fusible Web" on page 88 to trace the patterns for purses A, B, C, and D on pages 16–19 onto the paper side of the fusible web. Apply the shapes to the fabrics indicated on the patterns and cut them out.

   Note: You may substitute the patterns for purses E, F, and/or G on pages 23–25 for purses A, B, C, and/or D.

2. Arrange the prepared appliqué shapes for one purse onto a pink dot 10½" square. Place the pieces in numerical order so that the finished purse shape is centered on the square. Follow the manufacturer's instructions to fuse the pieces in place. Repeat to make a total of four blocks.

Assembling the Quilt Top

1. Sew two purse blocks and three black striped 2" x 10½" pieces together as shown. Press the seam allowances toward the striped pieces. Make two.

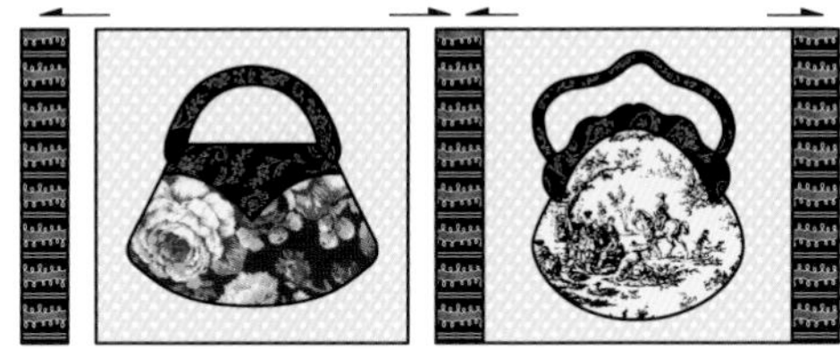

Make 2.

2. Sew three black-and-rose 2" squares and two black striped 2" x 10½" pieces together as shown to make a sashing row. Make three. Press the seam allowances toward the striped pieces.

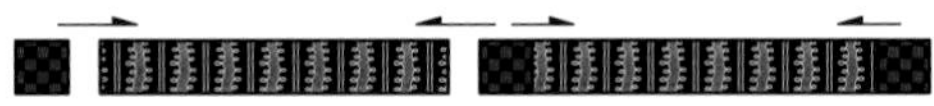

Make 3.

3. Sew the sashing rows and block rows together as shown to complete the quilt center. Press the seam allowances toward the sashing rows.

4. To add the inner border, sew a white-and-black 3¼" x 25" piece to the sides of the quilt center. Sew a paisley 3¼" square to the ends of the remaining two 3¼" x 25" pieces. Sew these units to the top and bottom of the quilt center. Press the seam allowances as indicated.

5. Refer to "Straight-Cut Borders" on page 89 to add the black 2½"-wide strips to the quilt top for the outer border.

Finishing Your Quilt

Refer to "Quiltmaking Basics" on page 88 for specific instructions regarding each of the following steps.

1. Layer the quilt top with batting and backing; baste—unless you plan to take your quilt to a long-arm quilter.
2. Hand or machine quilt as desired.
3. Use the black-and-pink floral 2¾"-wide strips to bind the quilt edges.
4. Refer to the photo on page 12 to center and hand stitch the beaded trim to the bottom of purse B, turning the ends under about ¼" to finish the edges. Embellish the purses with the buttons as desired.
5. Sew a hanging sleeve to the back of the quilt if desired.

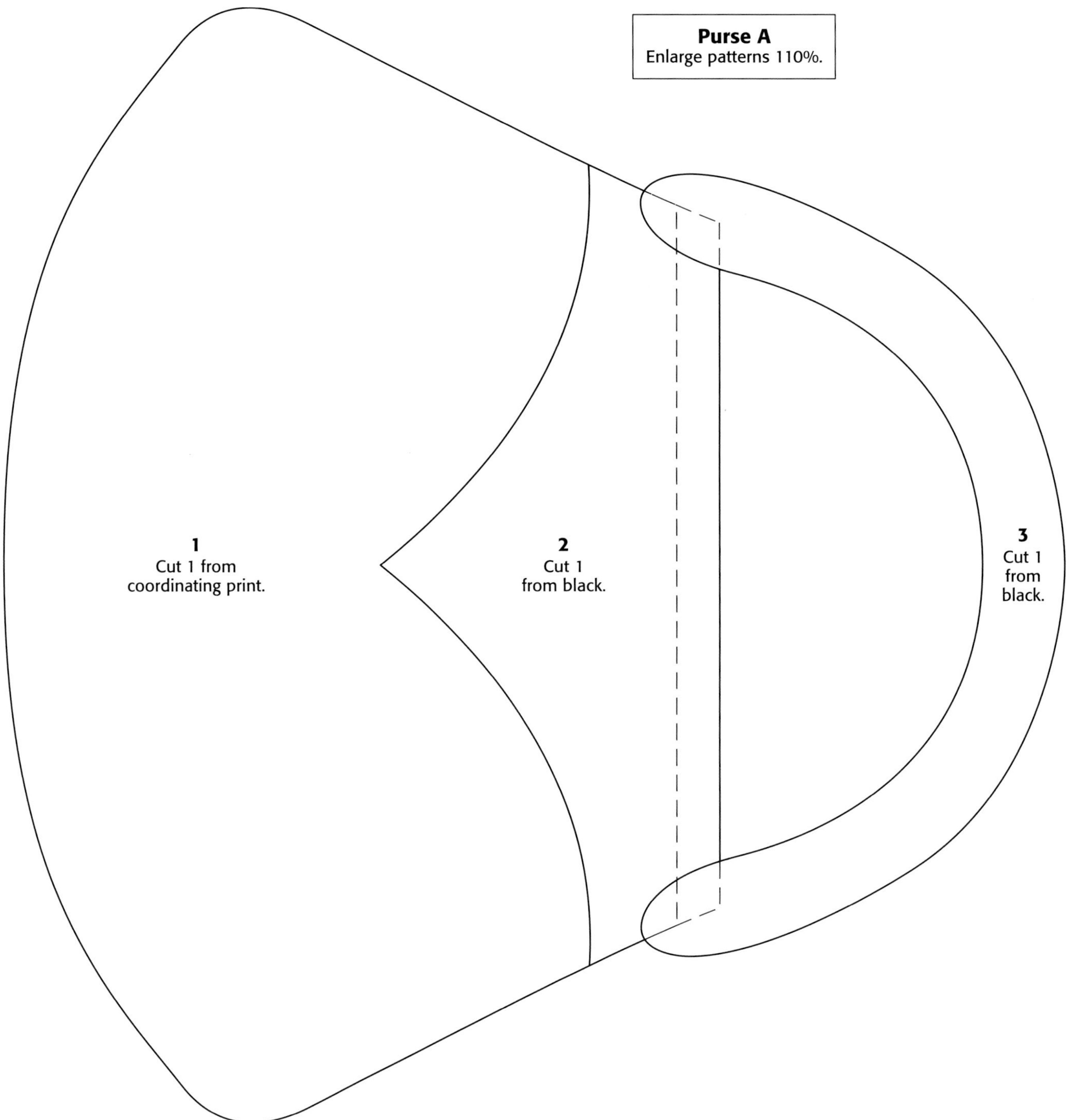
Purse A
Enlarge patterns 110%.
1
Cut 1 from
coordinating print.
2
Cut 1
from black.
3
Cut 1
from
black.

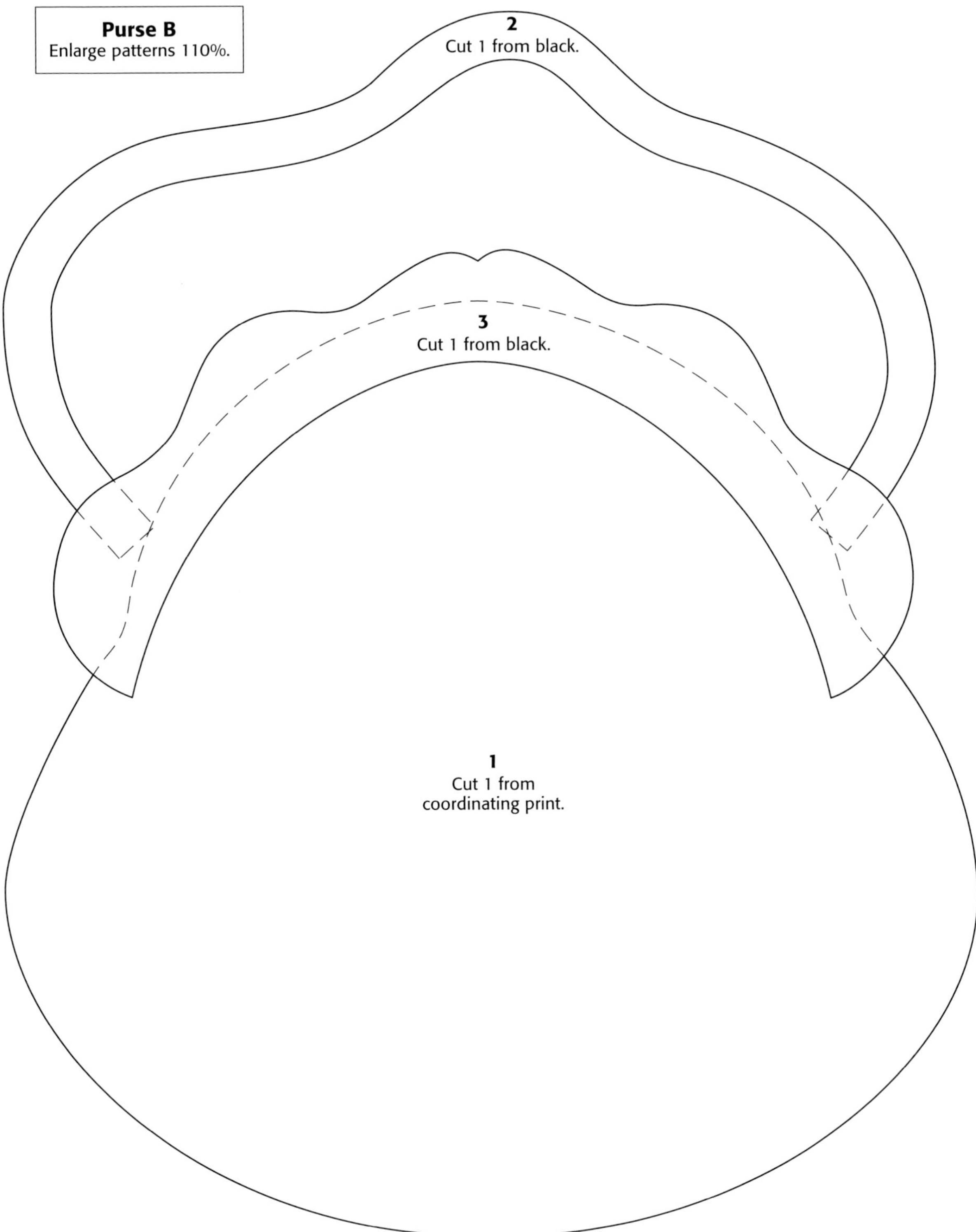
Purse B
Enlarge patterns 110%.
2
Cut 1 from black.
3
Cut 1 from black.
1
Cut 1 from
coordinating print.

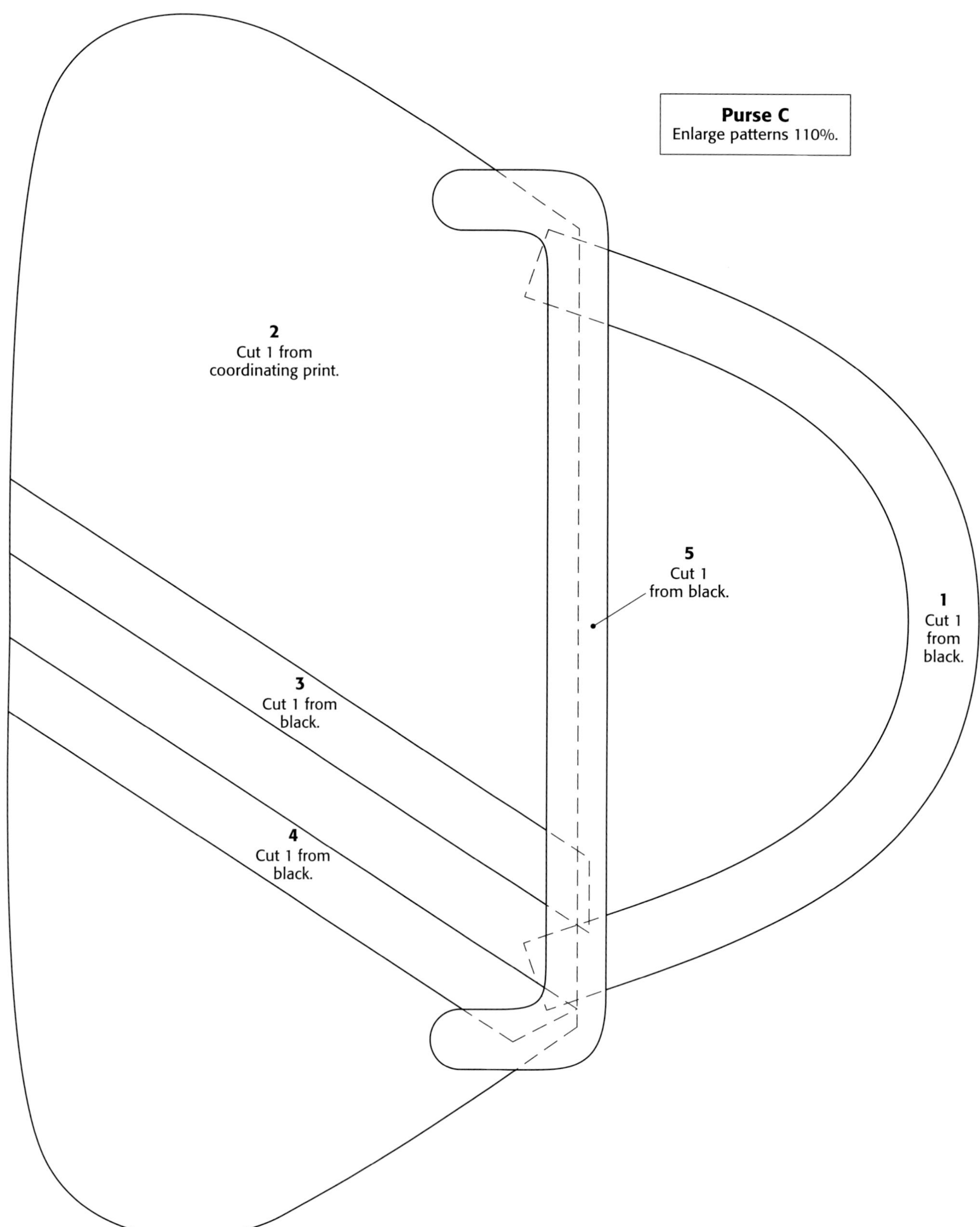
Purse C
Enlarge patterns 110%.
2
Cut 1 from
coordinating print.
5
Cut 1
from black.
1
Cut 1
from
black.
3
Cut 1 from
black.
4
Cut 1 from
black.

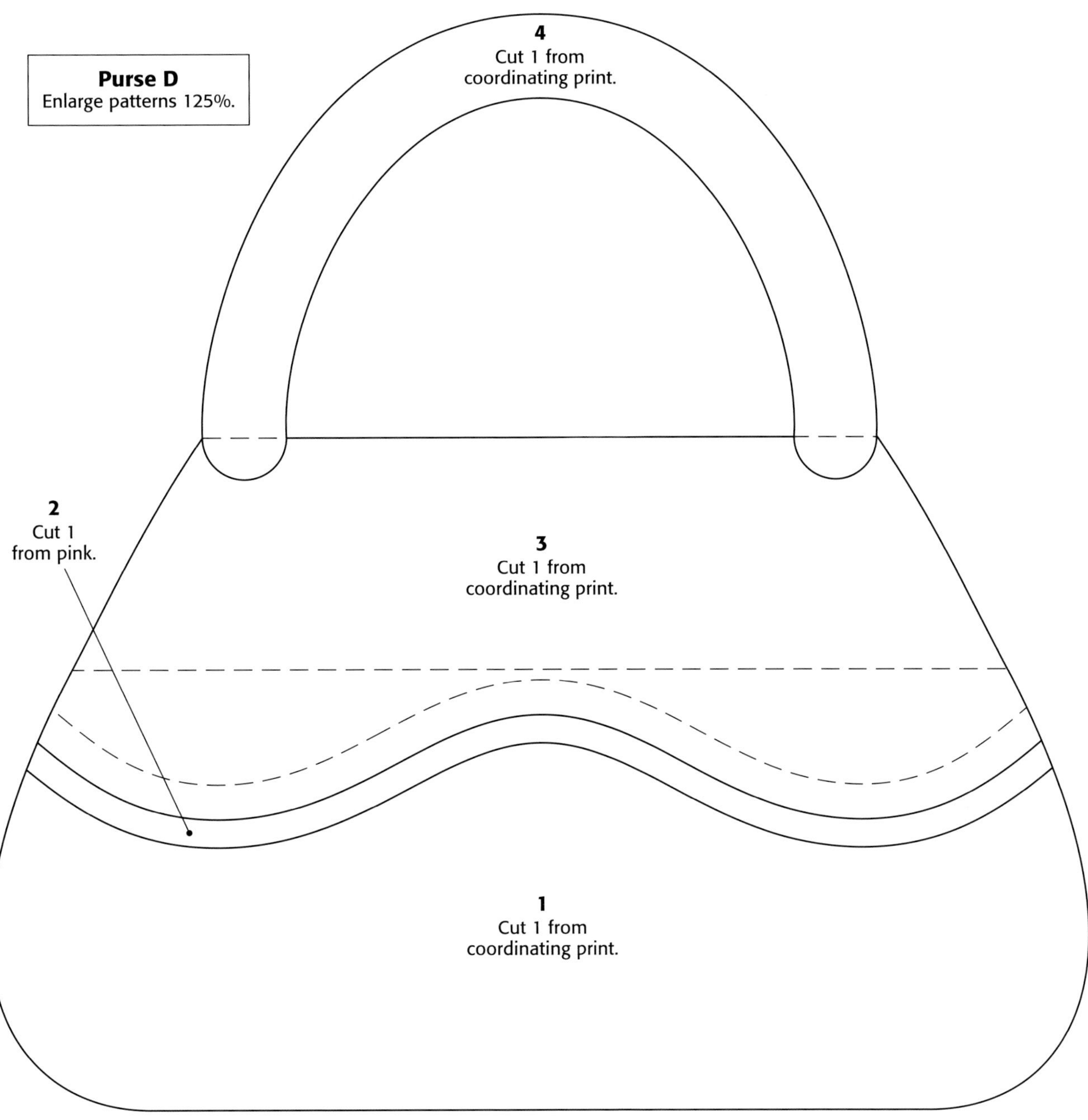
Purse D
Enlarge patterns 125%.
4
Cut 1 from
coordinating print.
2
Cut 1
from pink.
3
Cut 1 from
coordinating print.
1
Cut 1 from
coordinating print.

GRANDMOTHER'S PILLOWS

Skill level: *Confident beginner*

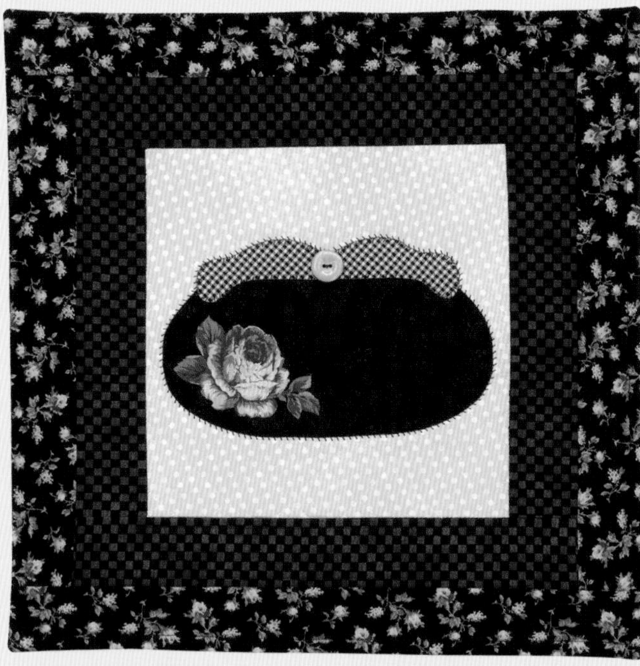

Finished pillow: 17½" x 17½"

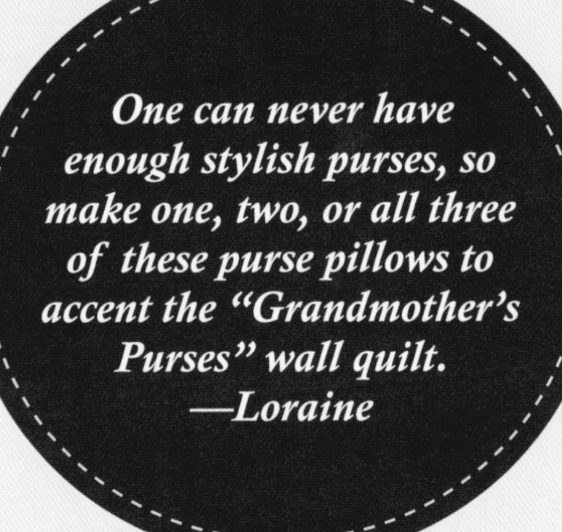

Button Box

It was great fun designing these purses, arranging the coordinating fabrics, and especially choosing the special buttons to accent each purse. Enjoy!

Materials (for one pillow)

Yardages are based on 42"-wide fabric unless otherwise noted.

¾ yard of muslin for block backing

⅜ yard of pink dot print for block background

½ yard of coordinating print for outer border and pillow back

¼ yard of 1 coordinating print for purse E or F appliqués, or ¼ yard *each* of 2 coordinating prints for purse G appliqués

¼ yard of black-and-rose check for inner border

¼ yard of black print for purse appliqués

22" x 22" piece of batting

⅓ yard of 17"-wide paper-backed fusible web

16" x 16" pillow form

12"-long zipper

Button(s) for embellishing

Cutting (for one pillow)

All measurements include ¼"-wide seam allowances.

From the pink dot print, cut:

- 1 square, 10½" x 10½"

From the black-and-rose check, cut:

- 2 strips, 2½" x 42"; crosscut into:
  - 2 pieces, 2½" x 10½"
  - 2 pieces, 2½" x 14½"

From the coordinating print for outer border and pillow back, cut:

- 2 strips, 2½" x 42"; crosscut into:
  - 2 pieces, 2½" x 14½"
  - 2 pieces, 2½" x 18½"
- 2 rectangles, 9⅞" x 18½"

From the muslin, cut:

- 1 piece, 22" x 22"

Making the Pillow Top

1. Refer to "Appliquéing with Fusible Web" on page 88 to enlarge and trace the patterns for purses E, F, and G on pages 23–25 onto the paper side of the fusible web. Apply the shapes to the fabrics indicated on the patterns and cut them out.

   Note: You may substitute the patterns for purses A, B, C, and/or D on pages 16–19 for purses E, F, and/or G.

2. Arrange the prepared appliqué shapes onto a pink dot 10½" square. Place the pieces in numerical order so that the finished purse shape is centered on the square. Follow the manufacturer's instructions to fuse the pieces in place.

   Note: If you want to add an appliqué to your purse, such as the one on purse F in the photo on page 20, apply paper-backed fusible web to the wrong side of the desired motif on a coordinating fabric. Cut out the motif and follow the manufacturer's instructions to fuse it in place on the front of the purse.

3. Sew the black-and-rose check 2½" x 10½" pieces to the sides of the block. Sew the 2½" x 14½" pieces to the top and bottom of the block.

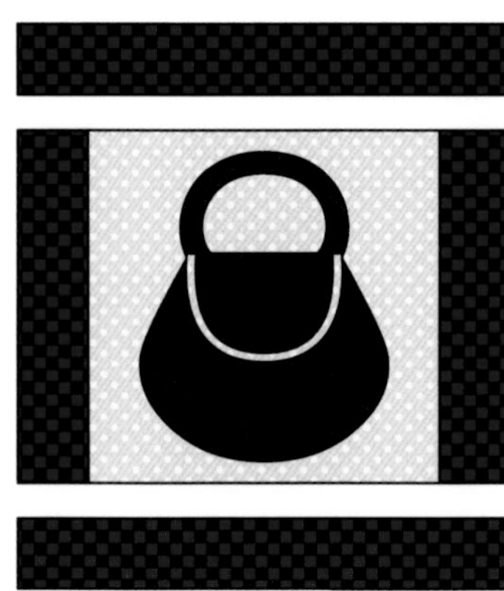

4. Sew the coordinating-print 2½" x 14½" pieces to the sides of the block. Then sew the coordinating-print 2½" x 18½" pieces to the top and bottom of the block.

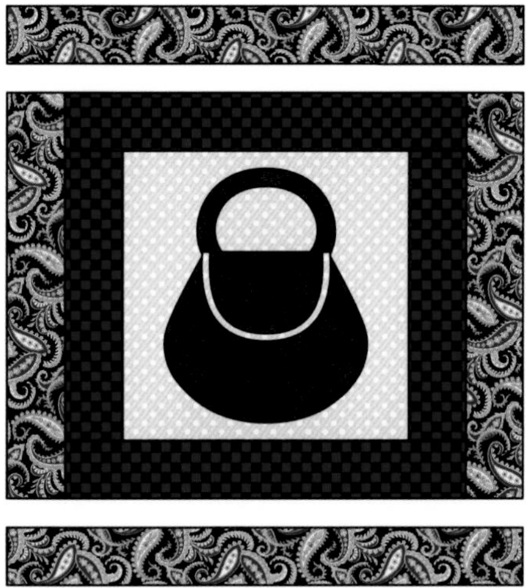

Quilting the Pillow Top

Refer to "Quiltmaking Basics" on page 88 for specific instructions regarding each of the following steps.

1. Layer the muslin, batting, and pillow top; baste, using thread or pins to hold the layers together.
2. Machine or hand quilt as desired.
3. Trim the excess batting and muslin even with the quilt top.

Assembling the Pillow

1. To make the backing, place the two 9⅞" x 18½" pillow-back rectangles right sides together. Pin-mark the beginning and end of a 12" section to mark the zipper placement. Using a basting stitch for the zipper area and a normal stitch length for the remainder of the seam, stitch ⅝" from the long edges. Press the seam open.

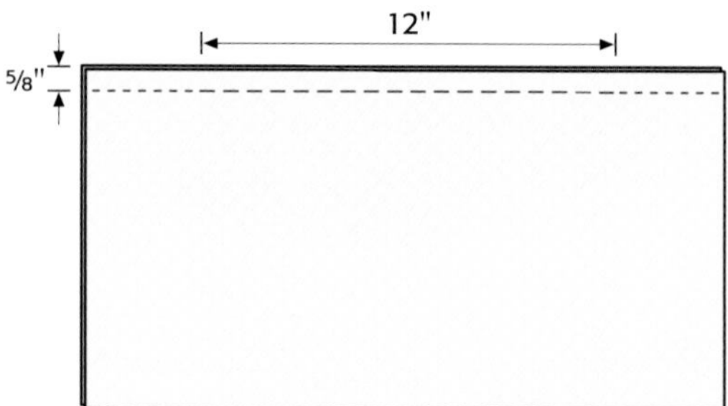

2. Follow the instructions on the zipper package to sew the zipper into place.
3. Place the pillow top and backing right sides together, aligning the raw edges. Pin the edges together. Sew completely around the pieces, using a ½" seam allowance. Clip the corners ¼" from the stitching to reduce the bulk.

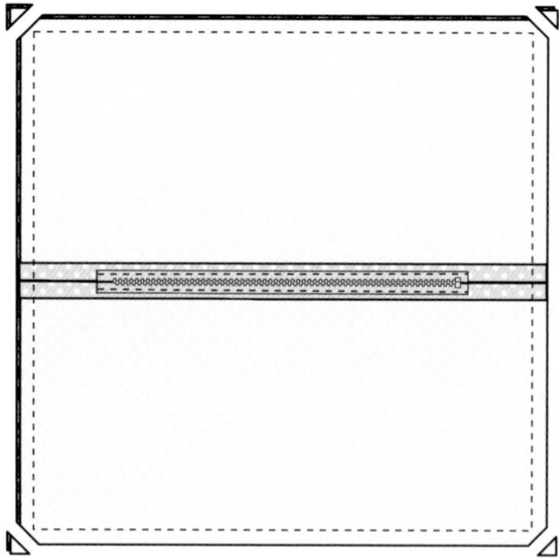

4. Turn the pillow cover right side out and press.
5. Topstitch ½" from the edges around the perimeter of the pillow cover, stitching through all layers.
6. Insert the pillow form.

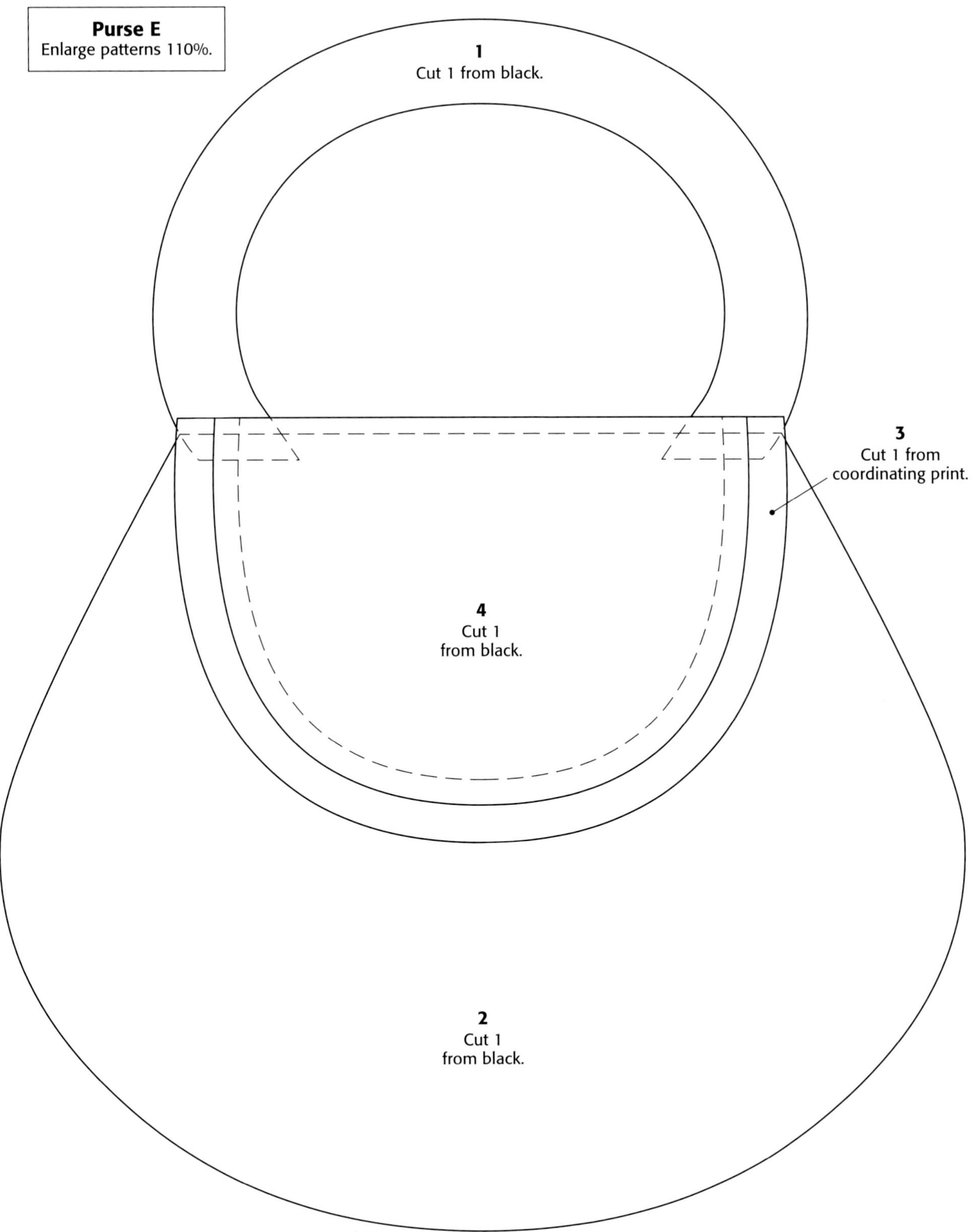
Purse E
Enlarge patterns 110%.
1
Cut 1 from black.
3
Cut 1 from
coordinating print.
4
Cut 1
from black.
2
Cut 1
from black.

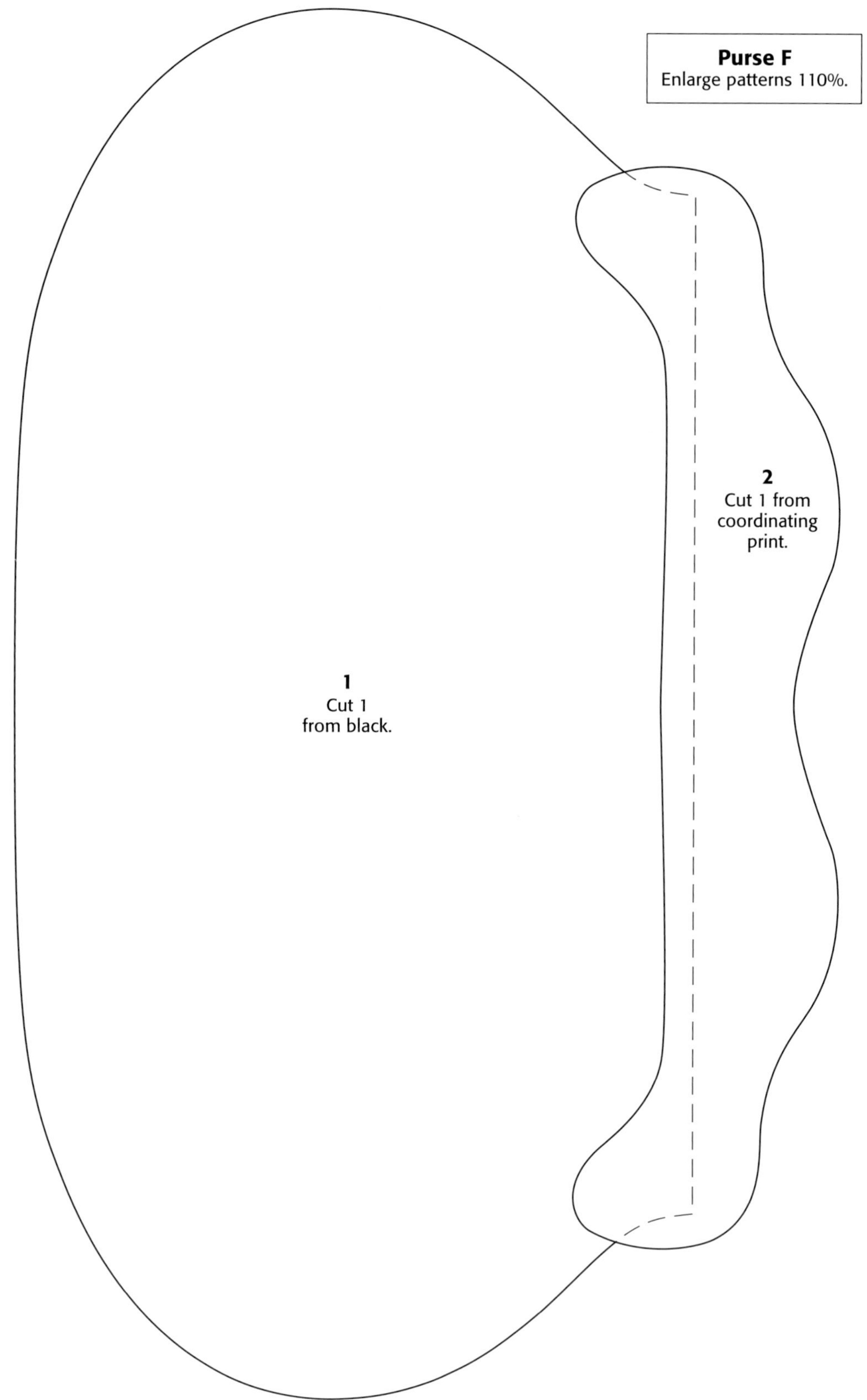
Purse F
Enlarge patterns 110%.
1
Cut 1
from black.
2
Cut 1 from
coordinating
print.

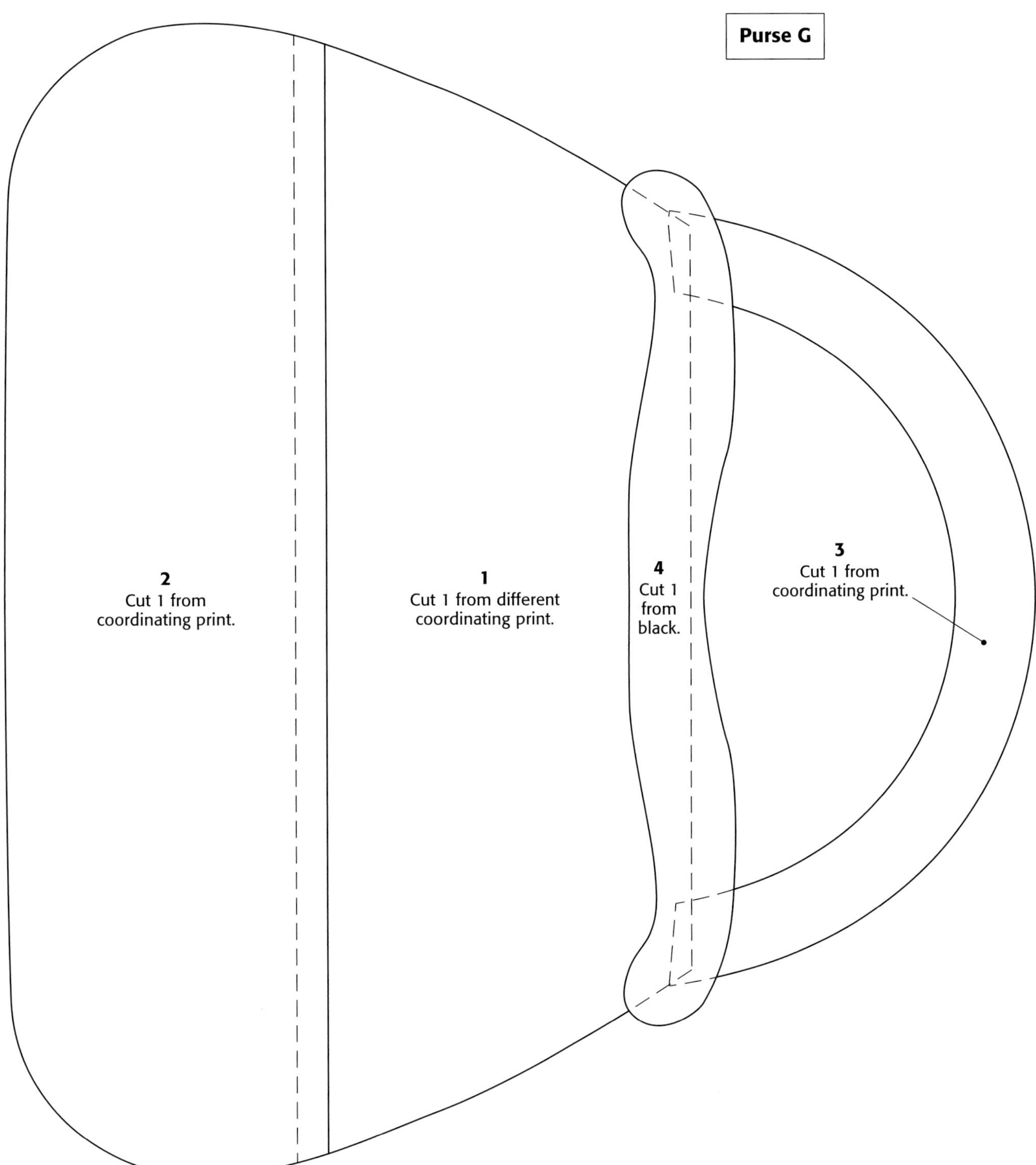
Purse G
2
Cut 1 from
coordinating print.
1
Cut 1 from different
coordinating print.
4
Cut 1
from
black.
3
Cut 1 from
coordinating print.

Going in Circles

Skill level: *Beginner*

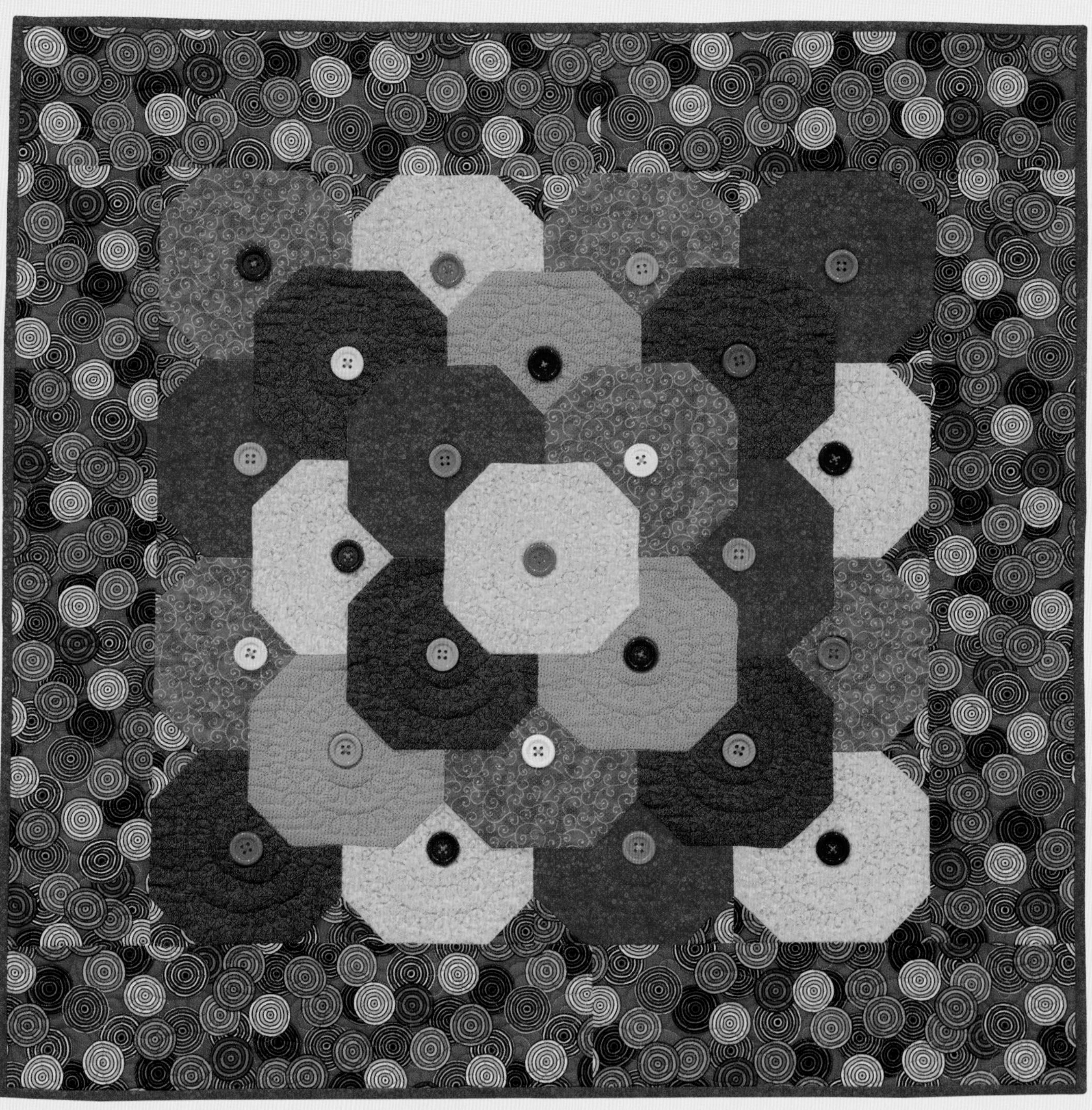

Finished quilt: 44½" x 44½"

Summertime meals of fresh corn on the cob and strawberry pie were served in my grandmother's kitchen on Fiestaware. This quilt is reminiscent of the collection of dinner plates from her cupboard.
—Susan

Button Box

In designing this quilt, I first found the fabulous border fabric that screamed "Buttons!" to me. Next, I found the big, bright buttons in a fabric shop. Then I designed the quilt to use the buttons with the dynamic button fabric. After completing the quilt and standing back from it, I discovered the Fiestaware!

Materials

Yardages are based on 42"-wide fabric.

1¼ yards of large-scale multicolored print for border

⅞ yard of red print for blocks and binding

½ yard of green print for blocks

½ yard of blue print for blocks

⅜ yard of yellow print for blocks

¼ yard of orange print for blocks

2¾ yards of fabric for backing

50" x 50" piece of batting

25 buttons, 1⅛" diameter, in colors to match block fabrics

Cutting

All measurements include ¼"-wide seam allowances.

From the yellow print, cut:

- 1 strip, 8½" x 42"; crosscut into:
  - 1 square, 8½" x 8½"
  - 5 rectangles, 4½" x 8½"
- 1 square, 4½" x 4½"
- 1 strip, 2½" x 42"; crosscut into 9 squares, 2½" x 2½"

From the red print, cut:

- 2 strips, 4½" x 42"; crosscut into:
  - 5 rectangles, 4½" x 8½"
  - 2 squares, 4½" x 4½"
- 1 strip, 2½" x 42"; crosscut into 8 squares, 2½" x 2½"
- 5 strips, 2¾" x 42"

From the green print, cut:

- 2 strips, 4½" x 42"; crosscut into:
  - 6 rectangles, 4½" x 8½"
  - 2 squares, 4½" x 4½"
- 1 strip, 2½" x 42"; crosscut into 10 squares, 2½" x 2½"

From the blue print, cut:

- 2 strips, 4½" x 42"; crosscut into:
  - 5 rectangles, 4½" x 8½"
  - 5 squares, 4½" x 4½"
- 1 strip, 2½" x 42"; crosscut into 5 squares, 2½" x 2½"

From the orange print, cut:

- 1 strip, 4½" x 42"; crosscut into:
  - 3 rectangles, 4½" x 8½"
  - 2 squares, 4½" x 4½"
- 1 strip, 2½" x 42"; crosscut into 4 squares, 2½" x 2½"

From the large-scale multicolored print, cut:

- 2 strips, 2½" x 42"; crosscut into 28 squares, 2½" x 2½"
- 5 strips, 6½" x 42"

Making the Units

1. Using a soft-lead pencil and a see-through ruler, draw a diagonal line from corner to corner on the wrong side of each 2½" square.
2. With right sides together, on the yellow 8½" square, position a red 2½" square on the upper left corner, a green 2½" square on the upper right corner, a blue 2½" square on the lower left corner, and an orange 2½" square on the lower right corner. Stitch on the diagonal lines. Trim ¼" from the stitching lines; press the triangles and the seam allowances toward the corners.

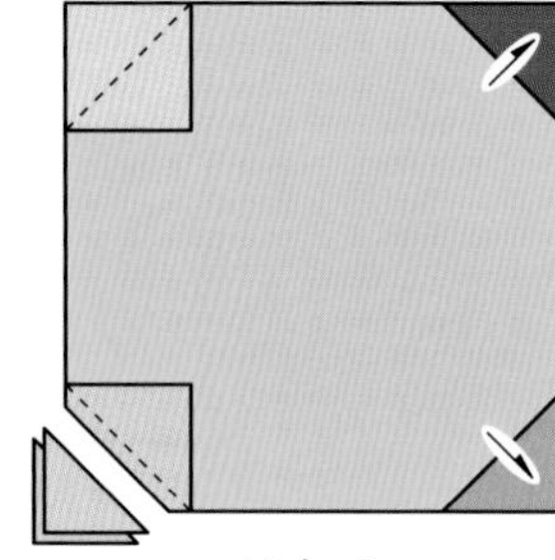

3. Following the step 2 stitching, trimming, and pressing sequence, place the 2½" squares on opposite upper corners of the 4½" x 8½" rectangles to make units in the color combinations shown.

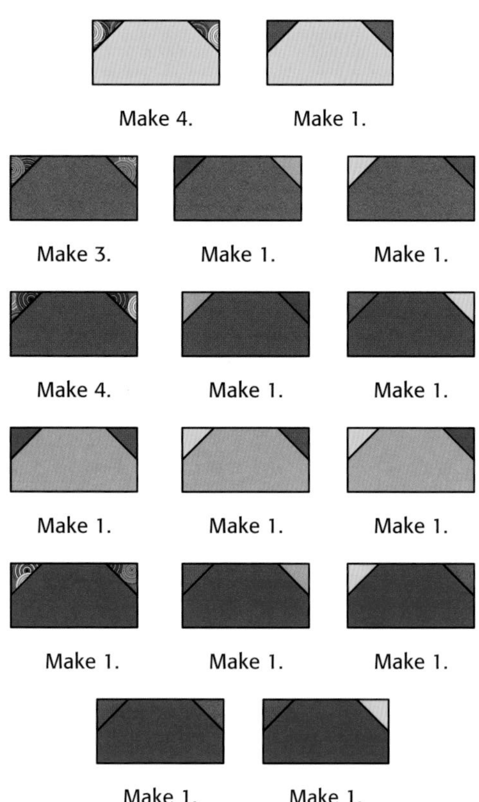

4. Using the same technique, place the 2½" squares on the upper left corner of the 4½" squares to make units in the color combinations shown.

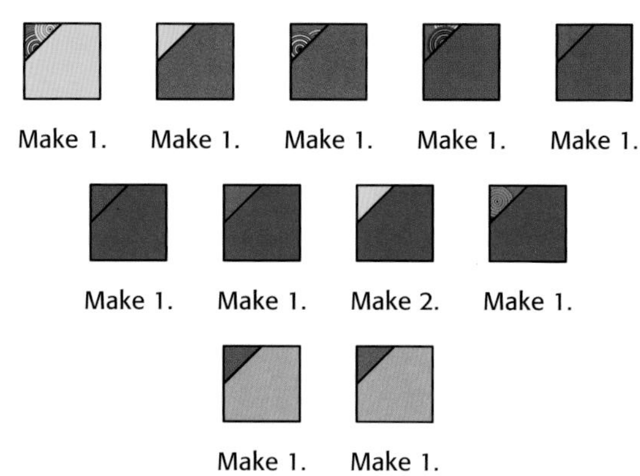

Assembling the Quilt Top

1. To make the quilt top, the units will be sewn together into three sections and then the sections will be sewn together. To make the center section, arrange and sew the appropriate colored units together as shown. Press the seam allowances in the directions indicated.

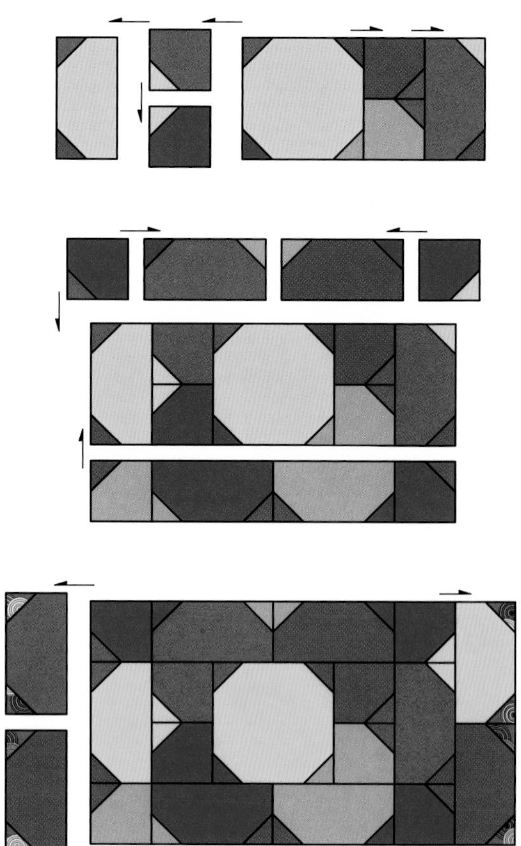

2. Arrange and sew the remaining units together to make the top and bottom sections as shown. Press the seam allowances in the directions indicated. Sew the sections together. Press the seam allowances in the directions indicated.

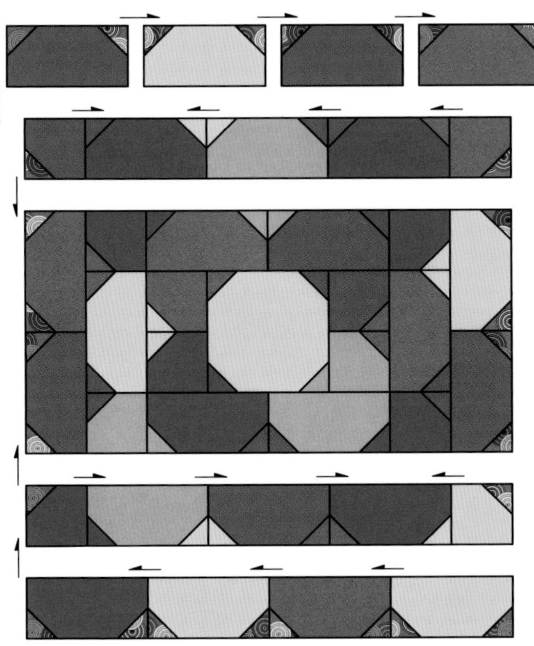

3. Refer to "Straight-Cut Borders" on page 89 to add the multicolored strips to the quilt top.

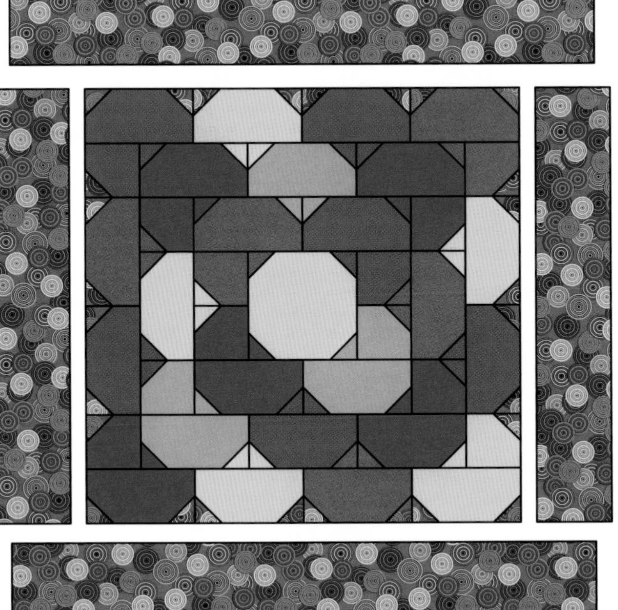

Finishing Your Quilt

Refer to "Quiltmaking Basics" on page 88 for specific instructions regarding each of the following steps.

1. Layer the quilt top with batting and backing; baste—unless you plan to take your quilt to a long-arm quilter.
2. Hand or machine quilt as desired.
3. Use the red 2¾"-wide strips to bind the quilt edges.
4. Refer to the photo on page 26 to embellish your quilt with the buttons, or create your own arrangement.
5. Sew a hanging sleeve to the back of the quilt if desired.

Fun Fiestaware Facts

Fiestaware was introduced in 1936 at the Pittsburgh Pottery and Glass Show with five original colors: ivory, yellow, light green, red, and cobalt blue. Turquoise was added in 1937. During the 1950s, chartreuse, forest green, gray, rose, and medium green joined the Fiestaware family. Two more colors, antique gold and turf green, were added in the 1960s. Fiestaware production was discontinued in 1972 but began again in 1986. Its popularity continues today.

Rowan's Quilt

Skill level: *Confident beginner*

Finished quilt: 36" x 48" • **Finished block:** 6" x 6"

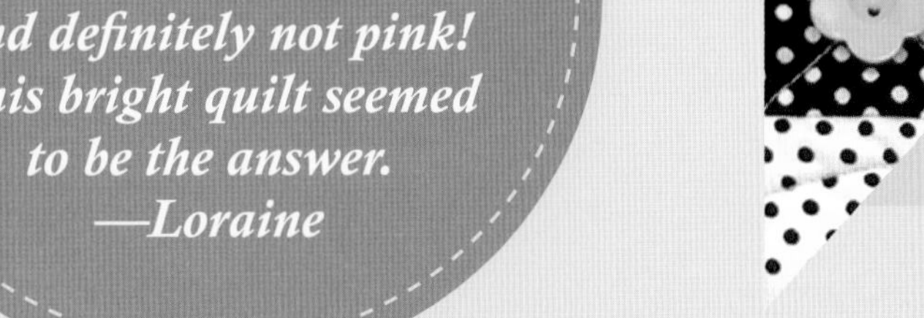

The challenge was to create a quilt for my second granddaughter that was girlish but not frilly, and definitely not pink! This bright quilt seemed to be the answer.
—Loraine

Button Box

I can never resist a beautiful button. The yellow flower buttons I used on this quilt waited in my button box for months before I made this quilt for Rowan.

Materials

Yardages are based on 42"-wide fabric.

1⅜ yards of yellow print for blocks and binding

1 yard of black-with-white dots print for blocks and border

1 yard of white-with-black dots print for blocks and border

1½ yards of fabric for backing

41" x 54" piece of batting

3 yards of black jumbo rickrack

2⅛ yards of white jumbo rickrack

17 yellow flower buttons, 1" diameter

Cutting

All measurements include ¼"-wide seam allowances.

From the yellow print, cut:

- 5 strips, 2½" x 42"; crosscut into 70 squares, 2½" x 2½"
- 6 strips, 2⅞" x 42"; crosscut into 70 squares, 2⅞" x 2⅞". Cut each square once diagonally to yield 140 triangles.
- 5 strips, 2¾" x 42"

From the black-with-white dots print, cut:

- 4 strips, 2½" x 42"; crosscut into 53 squares, 2½" x 2½"
- 3 strips, 2⅞" x 42"; crosscut into 36 squares, 2⅞" x 2⅞". Cut each square once diagonally to yield 72 triangles.
- 2 strips, 3¼" x 42"

From the white-with-black dots print, cut:

- 4 strips, 2½" x 42"; crosscut into 52 squares, 2½" x 2½"
- 3 strips, 2⅞" x 42"; crosscut into 34 squares, 2⅞" x 2⅞". Cut each square once diagonally to yield 68 triangles.
- 3 strips, 3¼" x 42"

Making the Blocks

1. To make block A, with right sides together, sew a yellow triangle to a black-with-white dots triangle as shown to make a triangle-square unit. Press the seam allowance toward the black triangle. Trim off the extended triangles. Repeat to make a total of 72 units.

Make 72.

2. Sew a yellow square between two triangle-square units from step 1 as shown. Press the seam allowances toward the yellow square. Repeat to make a total of 36 units.

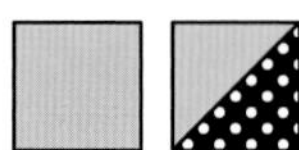
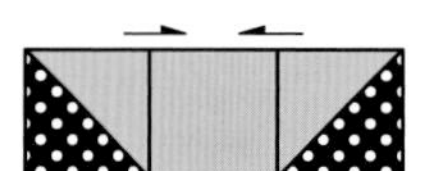

Make 36.

3. Sew a white-with-black dots square between two black-with-white dots squares as shown. Press the seam allowances toward the black squares. Repeat to make a total of 18 units.

Make 18.

4. Arrange two units from step 2 and one unit from step 3 into three horizontal rows as shown to complete block A. Press the seam allowances away from the center row. Repeat to make a total of 18 block A.

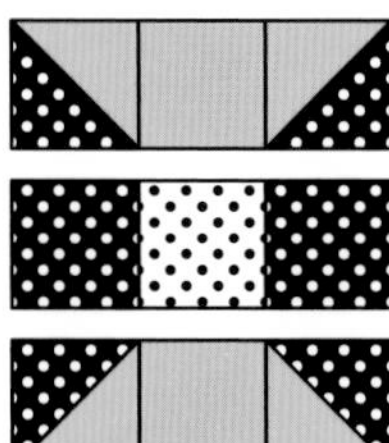
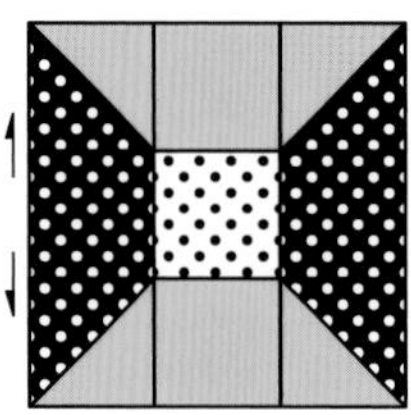

Block A.
Make 18.

5. To make block B, with right sides together, sew a yellow triangle to a white-with-black dots triangle as shown to make a triangle-square unit. Press the seam allowance toward the white triangle. Trim off the extended triangles. Repeat to make a total of 68 units.

Make 68.

6. Sew a yellow square between two triangle-square units from step 5 as shown. Press the seam allowances toward the yellow square. Repeat to make a total of 34 units.

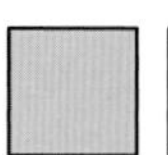
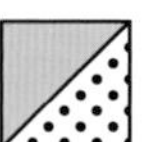
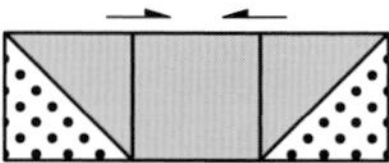

Make 34.

7. Sew a black-with-white dots square between two white-with-black dots squares as shown. Press the seam allowances toward the white squares. Repeat to make a total of 17 units.

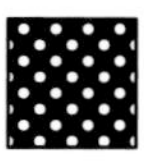
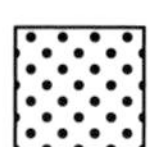

Make 17.

8. Arrange two units from step 6 and one unit from step 7 into three horizontal rows as shown to complete block B. Press the seam allowances toward the center row. Make a total of 17 block B.

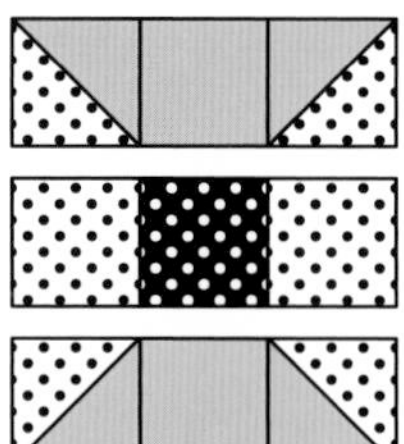
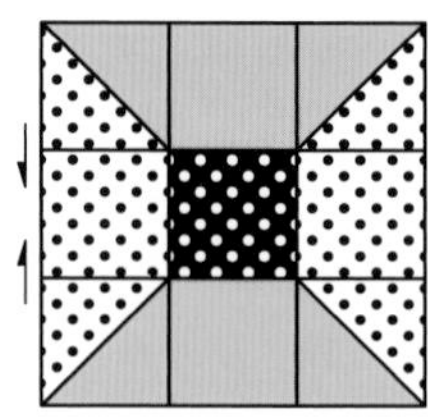

Block B.
Make 17.

Assembling the Quilt Top

1. Arrange the blocks into seven horizontal rows as shown, alternating the position of blocks A and B in each row and from row to row as shown. Sew the blocks in each row together, pressing the seam allowances in opposite directions from row to row. Join the rows. Press the seam allowances in one direction.
2. Refer to "Mitered Borders" on page 90 to add the 3¼"-wide border strips to the quilt. Place the white pieces on the sides of the quilt, and the black pieces on the top and bottom of the quilt.

Finishing Your Quilt

Refer to "Quiltmaking Basics" on page 88 for specific instructions regarding each of the following steps.

1. Layer the quilt top with batting and backing; baste—unless you plan to take your quilt to a long-arm quilter.
2. Hand or machine quilt as desired.
3. If desired, add rickrack to the border edges (see the photo on page 30 for detail). Sew the black rickrack along the sides of the quilt and the white rickrack along the top and bottom of the quilt. Half of the rickrack will be covered by the binding.
4. Use the yellow 2¾"-wide strips to bind the quilt edges.
5. Embellish your quilt with the flower buttons as shown in the photo on page 30, or create your own arrangement.

Just Buttons

Skill level: *Beginner*

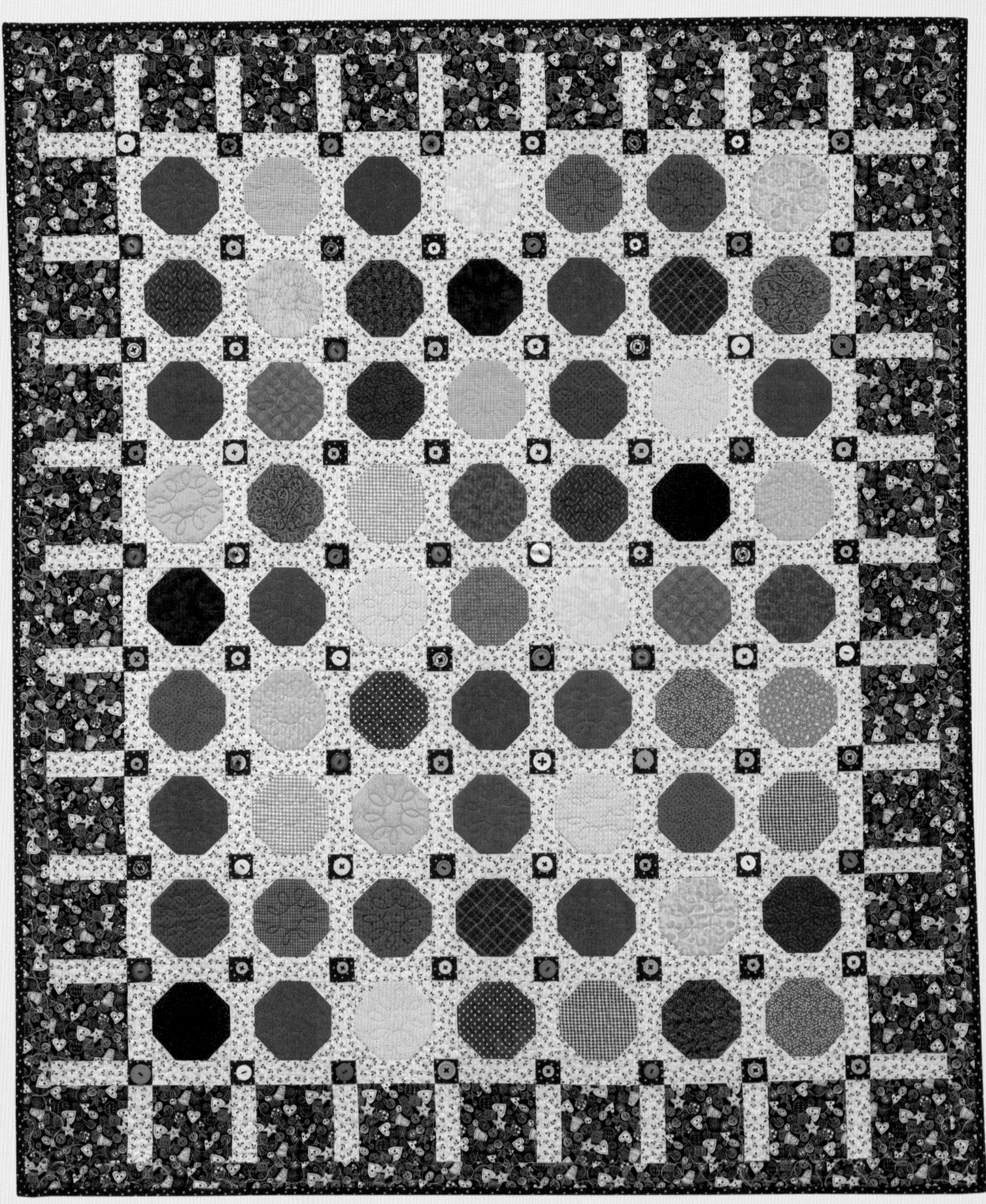

Finished quilt: 49½" x 60" • **Finished block:** 4" x 4"

When I was a little girl, buttons were sold individually. Stores kept the loose buttons in drawers that were divided into small sections. We could pull open the drawer to find the exact button we wanted. This quilt reminds me of the little compartments that were so fun to sift through as we looked for our favorites.
—Susan

Button Box

This quilt is literally a quilted button box filled with buttons of all colors. No two buttons need to be alike. The greater the variety of fabrics and buttons, the better. I dare you to find 80 different buttons to add to the cornerstones!

Materials

Yardages are based on 42"- wide fabric.

2 yards of cream print for block backgrounds, sashing, and inner border

1¼ yards of assorted medium and dark prints for Button blocks

1⅛ yards of multicolored print for inner and outer borders

⅞ yard of black print for sashing cornerstones and binding

3⅛ yards of fabric for backing

56" x 66" piece of batting

80 bright-colored buttons, ⅝" to 1⅛" diameter

Cutting

All measurements include ¼"-wide seam allowances.

From the cream print, cut:

- 9 strips, 4½" x 42"; crosscut into 178 pieces, 1¾" x 4½"
- 12 strips, 1¾" x 42", crosscut into 252 squares, 1¾" x 1¾"

From the assorted medium and dark prints, cut a *total* of:

- 63 squares, 4½" x 4½"

From the black print, cut:

- 4 strips, 1¾" x 42"; crosscut into 80 squares, 1¾" x 1¾"
- 6 strips, 2¾" x 42"

From the multicolored print, cut:

- 5 strips, 4½" x 42"; crosscut into 36 squares, 4½" x 4½"
- 6 strips, 2" x 42"

Making the Blocks

1. Using a soft-lead pencil and a see-through ruler, draw a diagonal line from corner to corner on the wrong side of each cream square.
2. With right sides together, position a cream square on each corner of an assorted-print square. Stitch on the diagonal lines. Trim ¼" from the stitching lines; press the triangles and the seam allowances toward the corners. Repeat to make a total of 63 Button blocks.

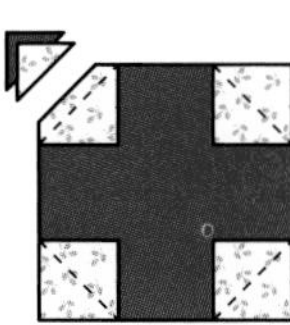
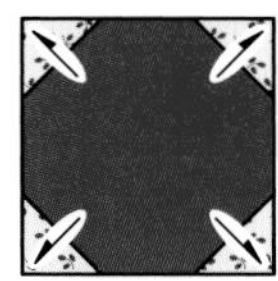

Make 63.

Assembling the Quilt Top

1. Randomly arrange the Button blocks between the cream 1¾" x 4½" pieces to create nine block rows. Add a multicolored 4½" square to the ends of each row. This will create the side inner borders when the rows are sewn together. Rearrange the Button blocks as needed to create a pleasing overall arrangement. Sew the pieces in each row together. Press the seam allowances toward the cream pieces.

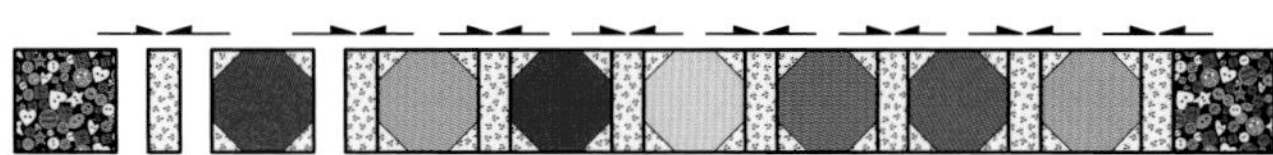

Make 9.

2. To make the sashing rows, sew eight black 1¾" squares between nine cream 1¾" x 4½" pieces as shown. Press the seam allowances toward the cream pieces. Make 10 sashing rows.

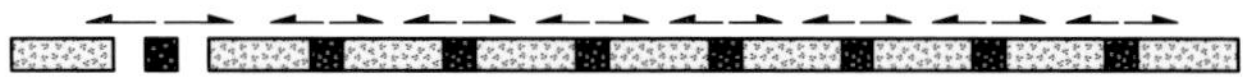

Make 10.

3. To make the top and bottom inner-border rows, sew eight cream 1¾" x 4½" pieces between nine multicolored 4½" squares. Press the seam allowances toward the cream pieces. Make two rows.

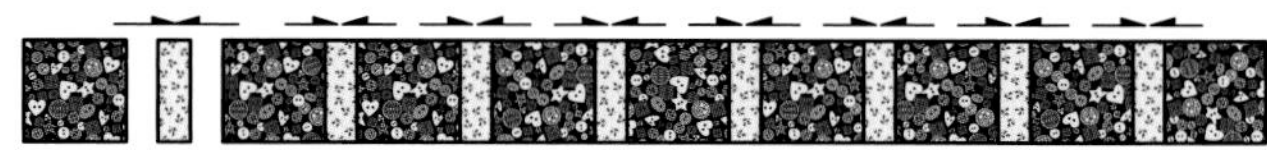

Make 2.

4. Following the previously determined arrangement, sew the block rows between the sashing rows. Add the top and bottom inner-border rows. Press the seam allowances toward the sashing rows.
5. Refer to "Straight-Cut Borders" on page 89 to add the multicolored 2"-wide strips to the quilt top.

Finishing Your Quilt

Refer to "Quiltmaking Basics" on page 88 for specific instructions regarding each of the following steps.

1. Layer the quilt top with batting and backing; baste—unless you plan to take your quilt to a long-arm quilter.
2. Hand or machine quilt as desired.
3. Use the black 2¾"-wide strips to bind the quilt edges.
4. Embellish each sashing cornerstone with a button as shown in the photo on page 34, or create your own arrangement.

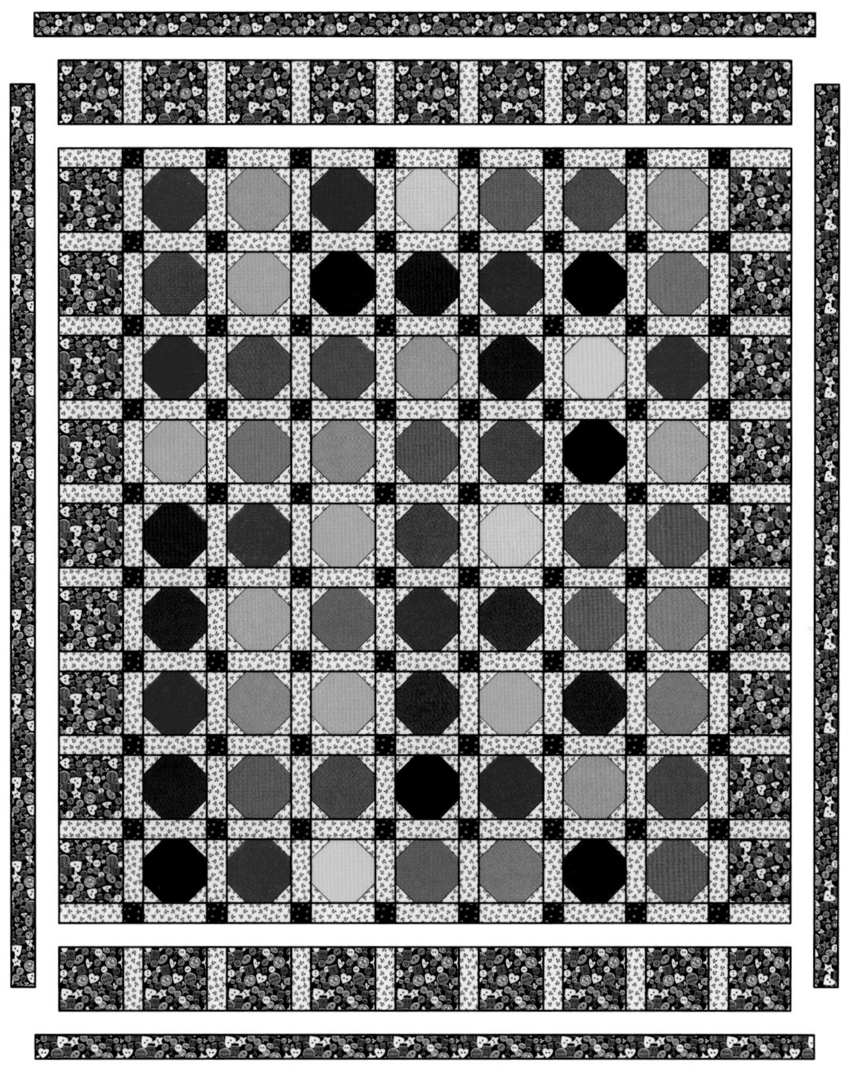

Soda Shop Hop

Skill level: *Confident beginner* 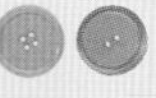

Finished quilt: 34¾" x 34¾"

Finished blocks: Ice Cream Sundae block: 8¾" x 10"

Banana Split block: 11¼" x 7½" • Ice Cream Cone blocks: 3¾" x 10"

Checkerboard block: 5" x 12½" • Ice Cream Soda block: 5" x 12½"

This wall quilt is a cool tribute to Mel's Drug Store and Soda Fountain, located in Idaho Falls, Idaho—and the wondrous ice cream confections found there on hot summer afternoons. Dish up these frozen treats in any flavor you wish. Add chocolate sauce, marshmallow cream, and cherries with no guilt whatsoever.
—Loraine

Button Box

The shiny, heart-shaped buttons on this quilt make the perfect cherries. I shopped for them, and when I didn't find just the right shade of red, I painted them with an enamel craft paint. Remember, anything goes!

Materials

Yardages are based on 42"-wide fabric unless otherwise noted.

1 yard of red print for sashing, inner border, outer border, and binding

½ yard of white-and-red print for appliquéd block backgrounds

⅜ yard of black print for Checkerboard block and pieced middle border

⅜ yard of white-and-black print for Checkerboard block and pieced middle border

⅓ yard of jade green for appliqués

Scraps of white, brown, yellow, light pink, dark pink, orange, light green, brown plaid, and red striped fabrics for appliqués

1⅓ yards of fabric for backing

42" x 42" piece of batting

1⅝ yards of 17"-wide paper-backed fusible web

7 red heart buttons, 1" diameter

Cutting

All measurements include ¼"-wide seam allowances.

From the black print, cut:

- 1 strip, 3" x 42"; crosscut into 5 squares, 3" x 3"
- 4 strips, 1¾" x 42"

From the white-and-black print, cut:

- 1 strip, 3" x 42"; crosscut into 5 squares, 3" x 3"
- 4 strips, 1¾" x 42"

From the white-and-red print, cut:

- 1 piece, 9¼" x 10½"
- 1 piece, 8" x 11¾"
- 2 pieces, 4¼" x 10½"
- 1 piece, 5½" x 13"

From the red print, cut:

- 5 strips, 1¾" x 42"; crosscut into:
  - 2 strips, 1¾" x 24¼"
  - 3 strips, 1¾" x 21¾"
  - 1 piece, 1¾" x 13"
  - 1 piece, 1¾" x 11¾"
  - 1 piece, 1¾" x 10½"
  - 1 piece, 1¾" x 9¼"
- 4 strips, 3¼" x 42"
- 4 strips, 2¾" x 42"

Sweet Treats

Speaking of confections, buttons are like candy to a quilter. My friend Pam always has a candy dish full of buttons to treat her friends with when they visit—special buttons for them to add to their collections.

Making the Blocks

1. To make the Checkerboard block, sew the black squares and the white-and-black squares into two rows as shown. Press the seam allowances toward the black squares. Join the rows. Press the seam allowance as indicated.

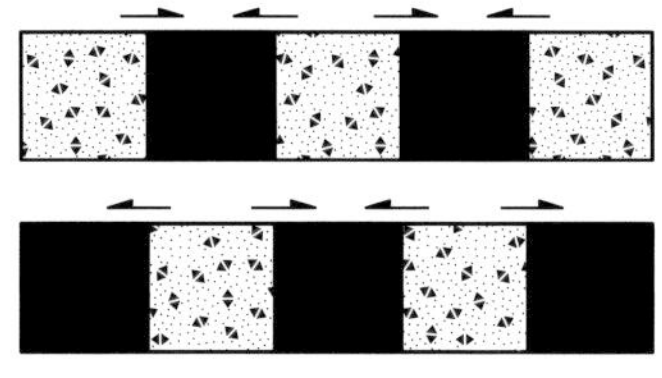

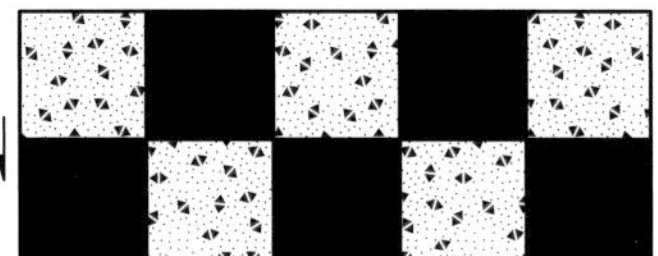

2. To make the appliquéd blocks, refer to "Appliquéing with Fusible Web" on page 88 to trace the patterns on pages 42–45 onto the paper side of the fusible web. (You will need to enlarge the ice cream soda pattern.) Apply the shapes to the fabrics indicated on the patterns and cut them out.
3. To make the Ice Cream Sundae block, arrange the prepared appliqué shapes on the white-and-red 9¼" x 10½" piece as shown. Place the pieces in numerical order so that the finished shape is centered on the rectangle. Follow the manufacturer's instructions to fuse the pieces in place.
4. Referring to the photo on page 38 as necessary for placement, repeat step 3 to complete the Banana Split block using the white-and-red 8" x 11¾" piece, and then complete the two Ice Cream Cone blocks using the white-and-red 4¼" x 10½" pieces. For the Ice Cream Soda block, arrange the prepared appliqué shapes on the white-and-red 5½" x 13" piece and fuse the shapes in place as before, except for piece 3 (straw). Fuse only the end of the straw that is in the glass in place and leave the remainder free. This will be fused in place after the inner border is attached.

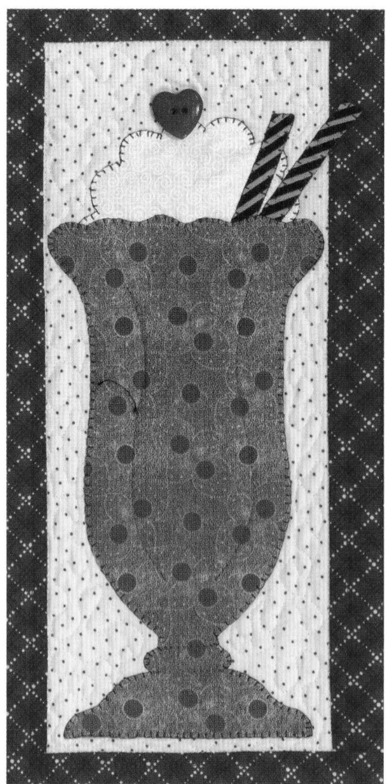

Assembling the Quilt Top

1. Sew the blocks, red sashing, and inner-border pieces together as shown to complete the quilt center, being careful to keep the straw of the Ice Cream Soda block out of the inner-border seam. Press the seam allowances toward the red pieces. Fuse the straw in place over the inner border.

2. To make the pieced border, sew a white-and-black 1¾"-wide strip to a black 1¾"-wide strip to make a strip set. Press the seam allowance toward the black strip. Repeat to make a total of four strip sets. Crosscut the strip sets into 84 segments, 1¾" wide.

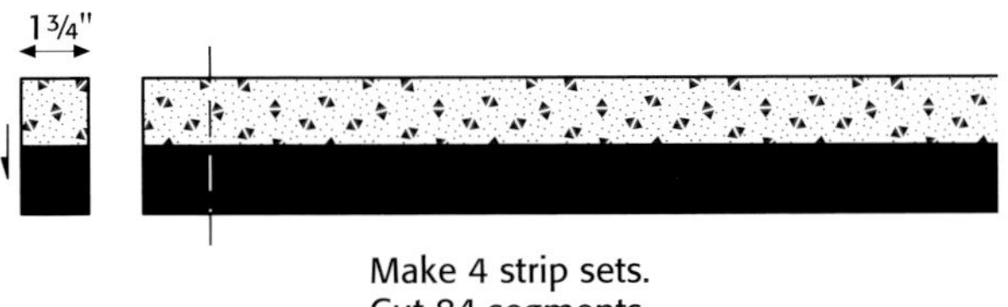

Make 4 strip sets.
Cut 84 segments.

3. Sew 19 segments from step 2 together as shown for the middle side borders. Make two rows. Sew these rows to the sides of the quilt center as shown. It is important to make sure the strips are oriented on the quilt correctly or the colors will not alternate when the top and bottom borders are added. Press the seam allowances toward the quilt center.

4. Sew 23 segments together as shown for the top and bottom borders. Make two rows. Sew these rows to the top and bottom of the quilt center as shown. Press the seam allowances toward the quilt center.

5. Refer to "Straight-Cut Borders" on page 89 to add the red 3¼"-wide strips to the quilt for the outer border.

Finishing Your Quilt

Refer to "Quiltmaking Basics" on page 88 for specific instructions regarding each of the following steps.

1. Layer the quilt top with batting and backing; baste—unless you plan to take your quilt to a long-arm quilter.
2. Hand or machine quilt as desired.
3. Use the red 2¾"-wide strips to bind the quilt edges.
4. Embellish your quilt by adding the red heart buttons to your ice cream confections.
5. Sew a hanging sleeve to the back of the quilt if desired.

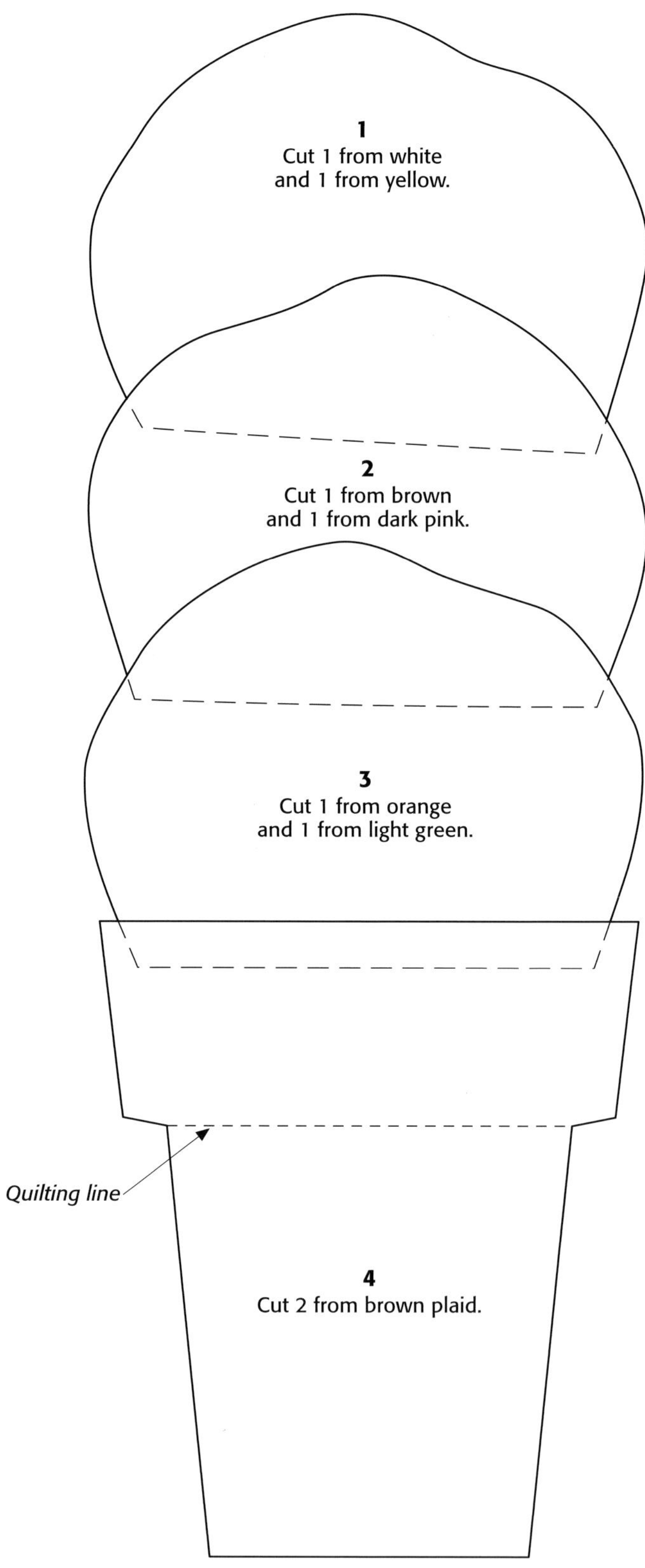

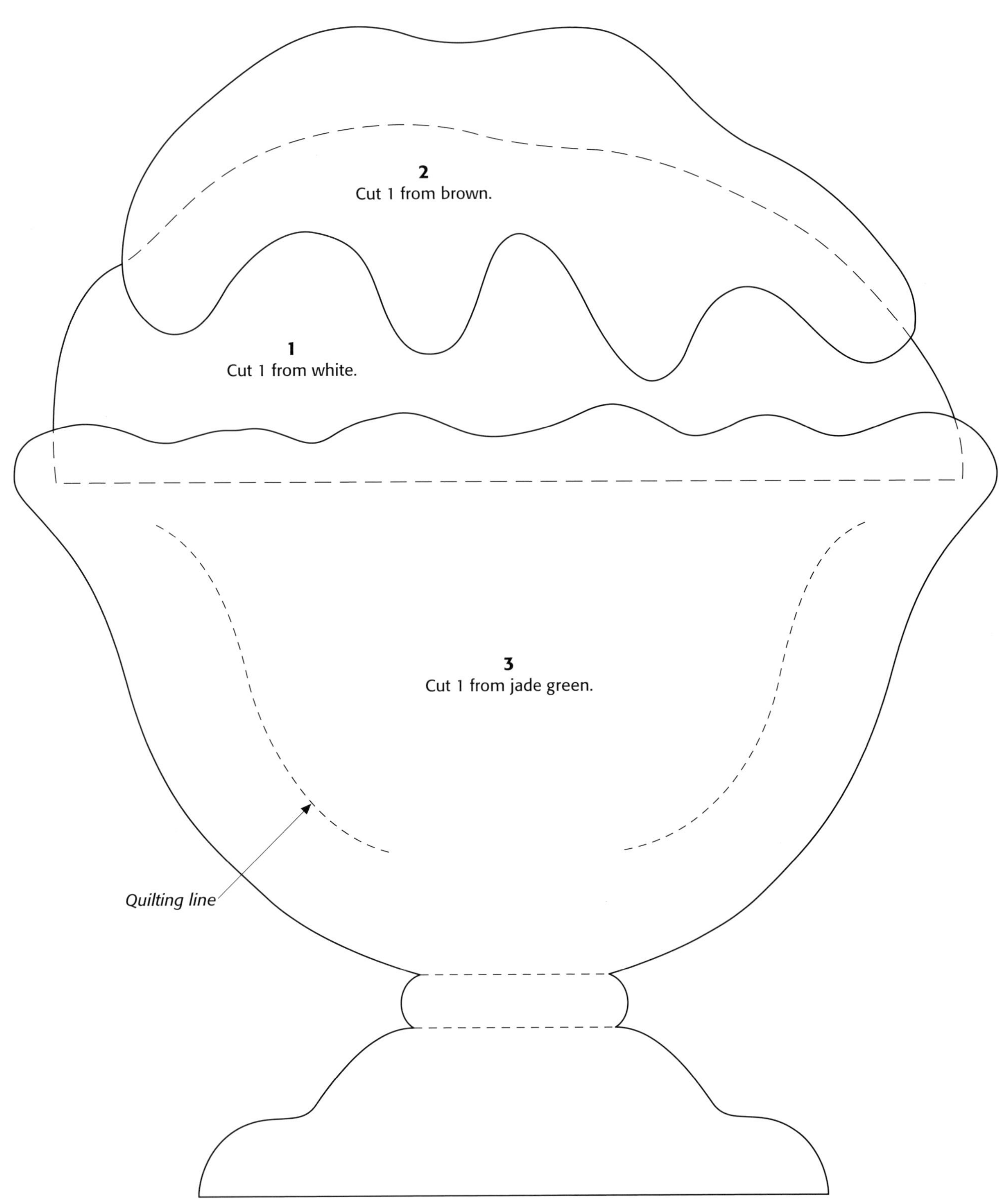
2
Cut 1 from brown.
1
Cut 1 from white.
3
Cut 1 from jade green.
Quilting line

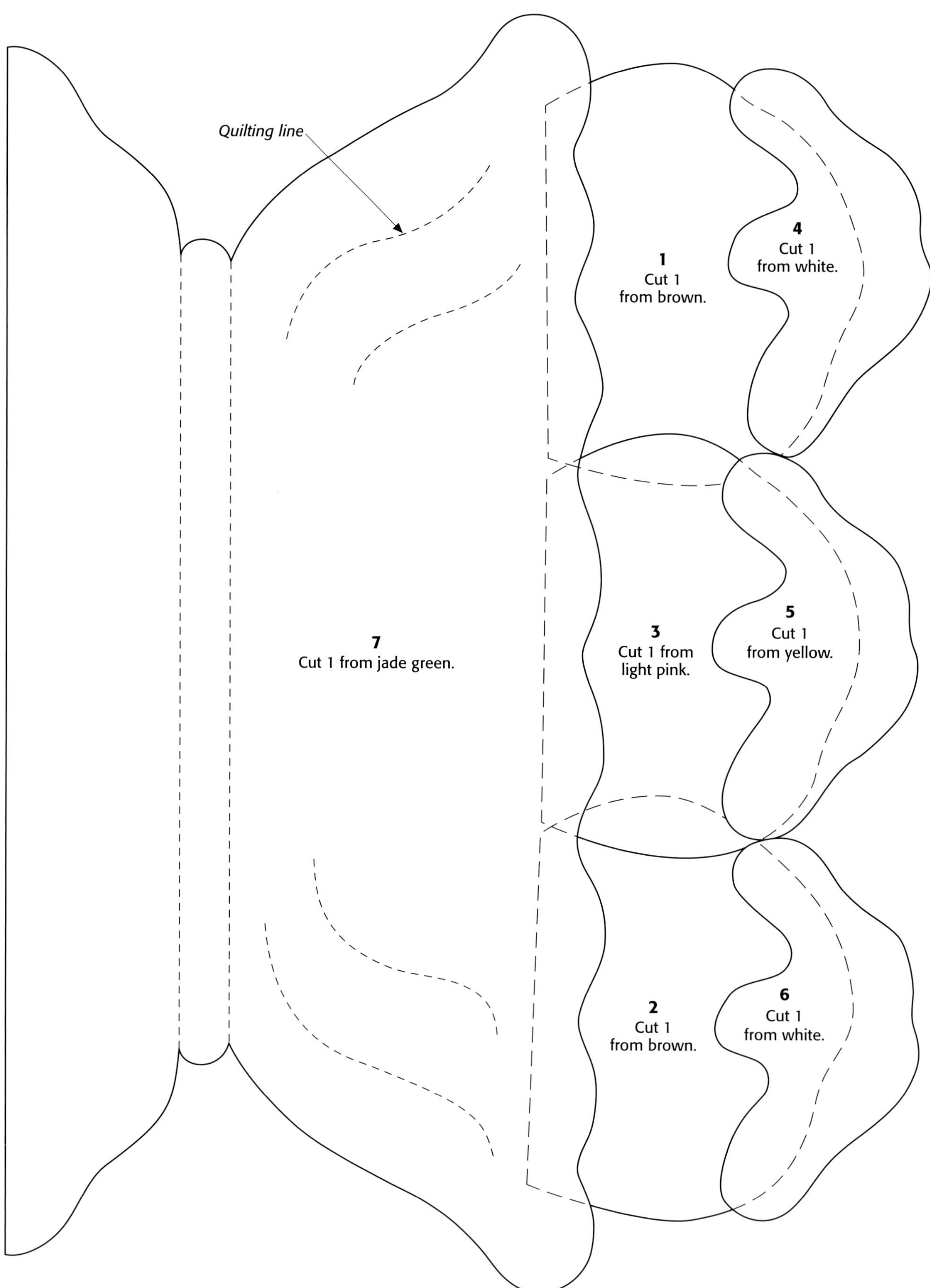
Quilting line
4
Cut 1
from white.
1
Cut 1
from brown.
7
Cut 1 from jade green.
3
Cut 1 from
light pink.
5
Cut 1
from yellow.
2
Cut 1
from brown.
6
Cut 1
from white.

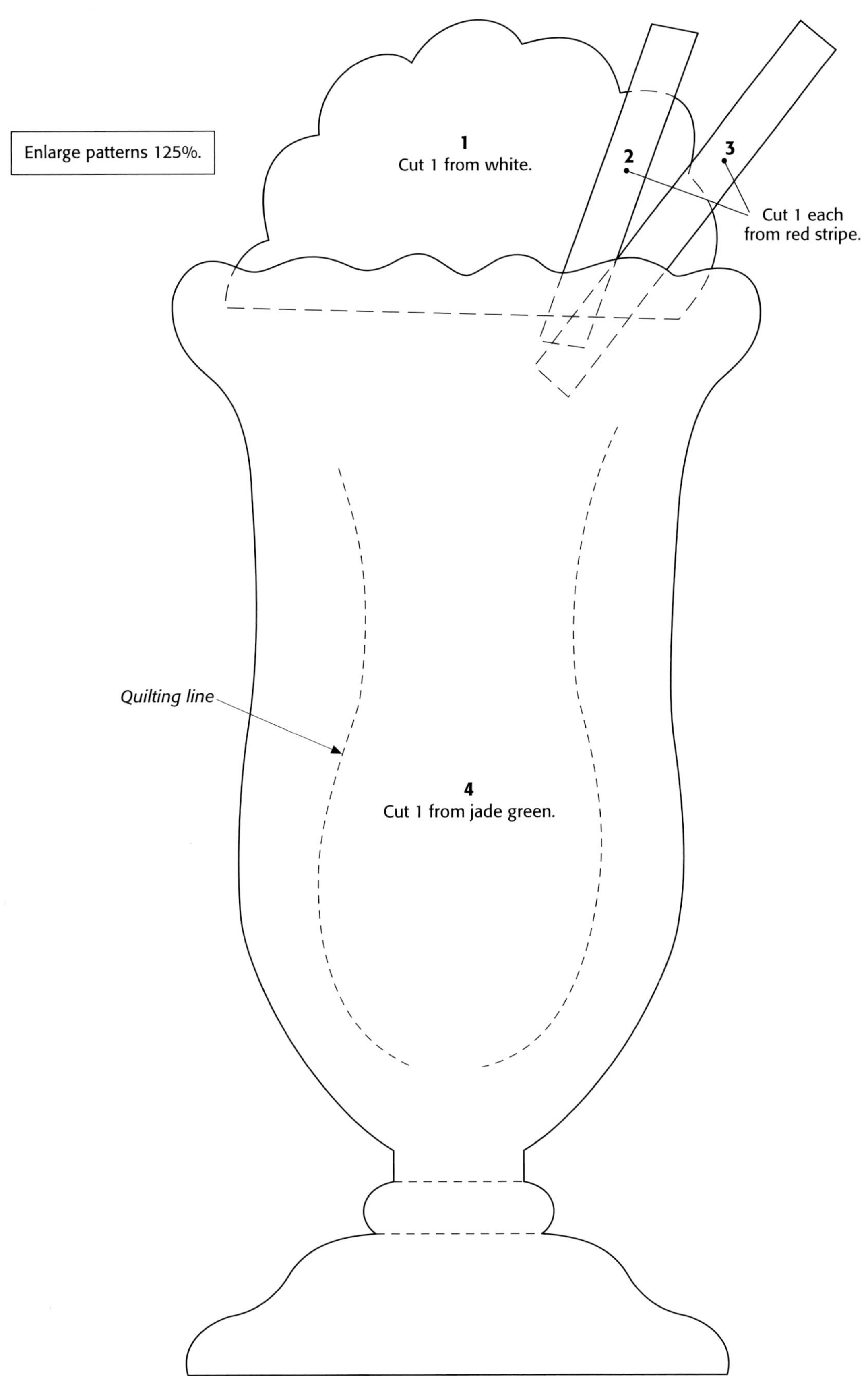
Enlarge patterns 125%.
1
Cut 1 from white.
2
3
Cut 1 each
from red stripe.
Quilting line
4
Cut 1 from jade green.

HAPPY TRAILS

Skill level: *Beginner*

Finished quilt: 40½" x 40½"

Finished blocks: Snowball and Chain blocks: 8" x 8"

Half block: 8" x 4" • Corner block: 4" x 4"

During the 1950s, cowboys were always taming the last of the Old West on the novel home-entertainment center: the television set. I was lucky enough to have grandparents who had ponies, so I could pretend to ride along with my favorite characters.
—Susan

Button Box

The silver conchos give this quilt a real Western saddle look and are attached with fabric strips. Conchos can be found at craft stores or saddle shops. Look closely for the pewter cowboy hats and boot buttons along the edges of the quilt center.

Materials

Yardages are based on 42"-wide fabric.

1⅓ yards of blue print for blocks, border, and binding

1⅛ yards of black print for Chain blocks, Chain half blocks, border, and concho ties

1 yard of red print for blocks and border

1¼ yards of fabric for backing

45" x 45" piece of batting

8 silver conchos, 1¼" diameter

8 pewter cowboy-theme buttons, 1" to 2" long

Cutting

All measurements include ¼"-wide seam allowances.

From the blue print, cut:

- 2 strips, 4½" x 42"; crosscut into 24 pieces, 2½" x 4½"
- 3 strips, 2½" x 42"; crosscut into 48 squares, 2½" x 2½"
- 4 strips, 2½" x 32½"
- 5 strips, 2¾" x 42"

From the red print, cut:

- 2 strips, 8½" x 42"; crosscut into:
  - 5 squares, 8½" x 8½"
  - 4 rectangles, 4½" x 8½"
- 4 squares, 4½" x 4½"
- 5 strips, 1½" x 42"
- 1 strip, 2½" x 42"

From the black print, cut:

- 1 strip, 12" x 42"; crosscut into 8 pieces, 2" x 12"
- 1 strip, 2½" x 42"
- 5 strips, 1½" x 42"
- 8 strips, 1½" x 32½"

Making the Snowball Blocks, Half Blocks, and Quarter Blocks

1. Using a soft-lead pencil and a see-through ruler, draw a diagonal line from corner to corner on the wrong side of each blue square.
2. With right sides together, place a blue square on each corner of a red 8½" square as shown. Stitch on the diagonal lines. Trim ¼" from the stitching lines; press the triangles and seam allowances toward the corner. Repeat to make a total of five Snowball blocks.

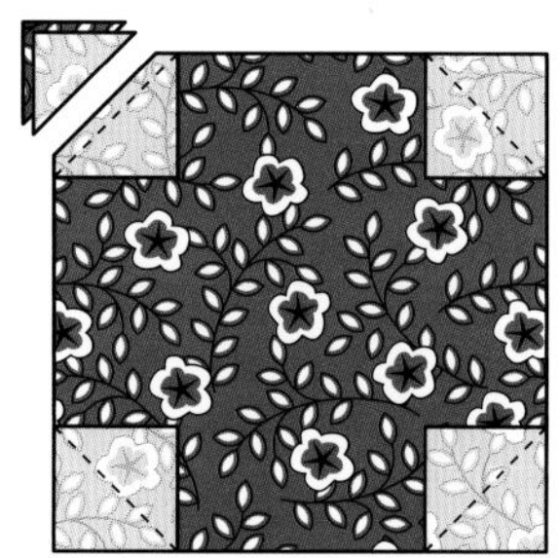

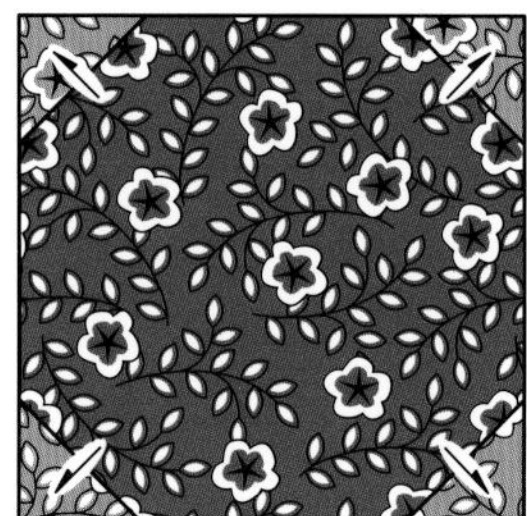

Snowball block.
Make 5.

3. Position a blue square on each upper corner of a red 4½" x 8½" rectangle as shown, right sides together. Stitch, trim, and press as instructed in step 2. Repeat to make a total of four Snowball half blocks.

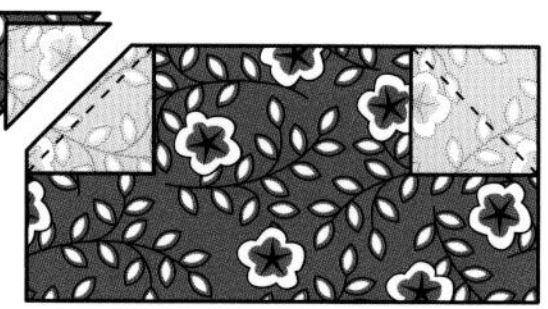

Snowball half block.
Make 4.

4. Place a blue square on one corner of a red 4½" square, right sides together. Stitch, trim, and press as instructed in step 2. Repeat to make a total of four Snowball quarter blocks.

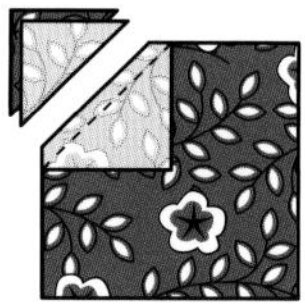

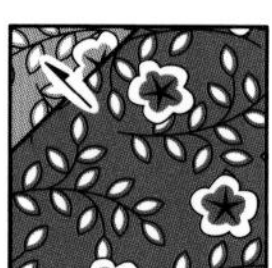

Snowball quarter block.
Make 4.

Making the Chain Blocks, Half Blocks, and Border Corner Blocks

1. Sew a red 1½" x 42" strip to a black 1½" x 42" strip as shown. Press the seam allowances toward the black. Repeat to make a total of three strip sets. Crosscut the strip sets into 64 segments, 1½" wide.

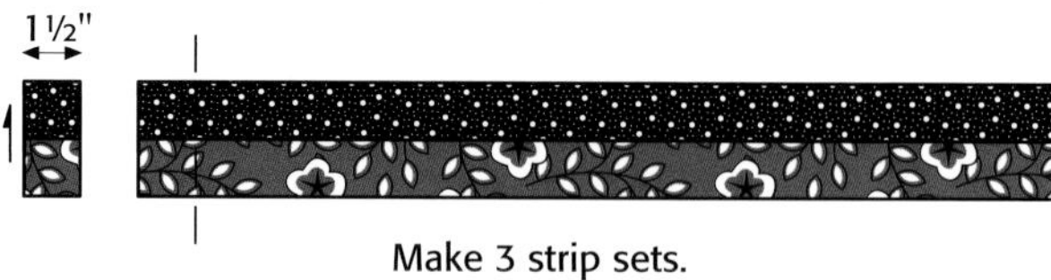

Make 3 strip sets.
Cut 64 segments.

2. Sew two segments from step 1 together as shown to make a four-patch unit. Press the seam allowance in either direction. Repeat to make a total of 32 units.

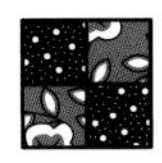

Make 32.

3. Sew the red 2½" x 42" strip between two black 1½" x 42" strips to make a strip set. Press the seam allowances toward the black. Crosscut the strip set into 24 segments, 1½" wide.

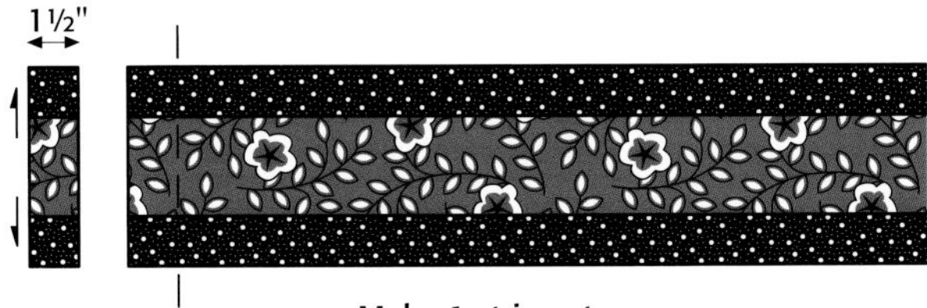

Make 1 strip set.
Cut 24 segments.

4. Sew a black 2½" x 42" strip between two red 1½" x 42" strips. Press the seam allowances toward the black. Crosscut the strip set into eight segments, 2½" wide, and eight segments, 1½" wide.

Make 1 strip set.
Cut 8 segments of each width.

5. Using segments from steps 3 and 4, make eight units as shown. Press the seam allowances as indicated. Set aside four of these units for the pieced border.

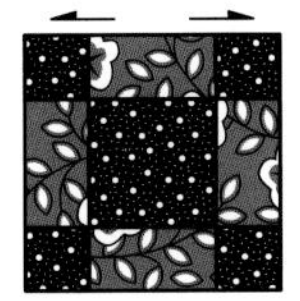

Make 8.

6. Use the remaining segments from steps 3 and 4 to make eight units as shown. Press the seam allowances as indicated.

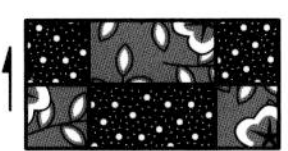

Make 8.

7. Arrange four blue 2½" x 4½" pieces, four four-patch units, and one step 5 unit into three rows as shown. Sew the pieces in each row together. Press the seam allowances as indicated. Sew the rows together. Press the seam allowances as indicated. Repeat to make a total of four Chain blocks.

Chain block.
Make 4.

8. Arrange one blue 2½" x 4½" piece, two blue squares, two four-patch units, and one unit from step 6 into two rows as shown. Sew the pieces in each row together. Press the seam allowances as indicated. Sew the rows together. Press the seam allowances as indicated. Repeat to make a total of eight Chain half blocks.

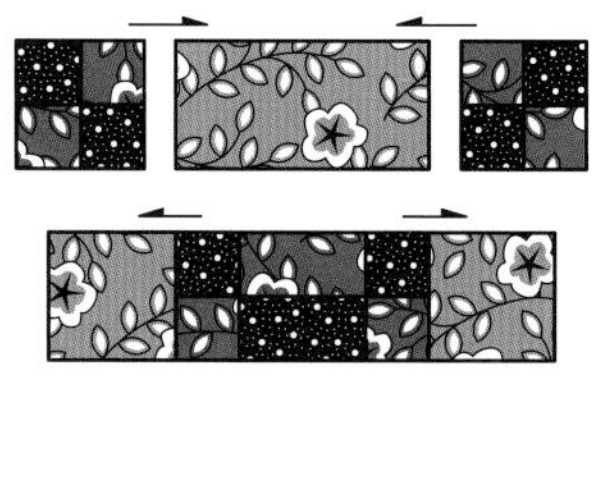

Chain half block.
Make 8.

Assembling the Quilt Top

1. Arrange the blocks into five horizontal rows as shown. Sew the blocks in each row together. Press the seam allowances in opposite directions from row to row. Join the rows. Press the seam allowances in one direction.

2. To make the pieced border strips, sew one blue 2½" x 32½" strip between two black 1½" x 32½" strips. Press the seam allowances toward the blue. Make four pieced border strips.

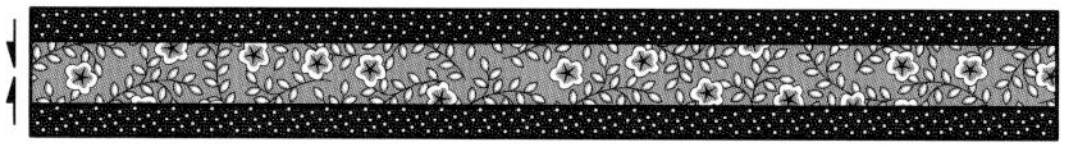

Make 4.

3. Sew a pieced border strip to opposite sides of the quilt top. Press the seam allowances toward the borders. Add a unit set aside when making the Chain blocks (step 5) to the ends of the remaining two pieced border strips. Press the seam allowances toward the border strips. Sew these strips to the top and bottom of the quilt top. Press the seam allowances toward the borders.

Finishing Your Quilt

Refer to "Quiltmaking Basics" on page 88 for specific instructions regarding each of the following steps.

1. Layer the quilt top, batting, and backing; baste—unless you plan to take your quilt to a long-arm quilter.
2. Hand or machine quilt as desired.
3. Use the blue 2¾"-wide strips to bind the quilt edges.
4. To make the ties for attaching the conchos, press the ends of each black 2" x 12" strip under ½". Fold the strips in half lengthwise, wrong sides together; press. Open the strips (don't unfold the ends) so they are wrong side up. Fold the raw edges in to meet the center folds and then fold the strips in half lengthwise again; press. Topstitch the strips along the double-folded edge. Position each strip on the quilt top where you want to place the conchos. Hand or machine stitch through the center of the ties. Slide the conchos onto the strips and tie in place.

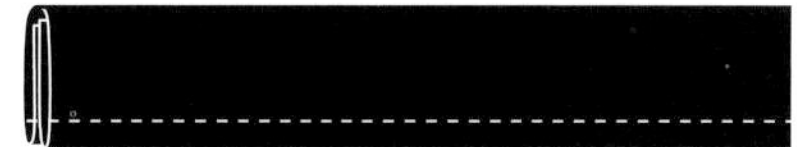

Topstitch double-folded edge.

5. Embellish the quilt with the cowboy-theme buttons as shown in the photo on page 46, or create your own arrangement.
6. Sew a hanging sleeve to the back of the quilt if desired.

Spinners

Skill level: *Confident beginner*

Finished quilt: 50" x 50" • **Finished block:** 8" x 8"

In the summertime, when tables are decked with brightly colored cloths and pinwheels appear in the backyard, we know it's time for a family picnic. Lively colors and plenty of pinwheels make this quilt the perfect complement to your outdoor decor.
—Loraine

Button Box

Just choose from what you have in your button box for this quilt. The buttons can vary in size, style, and color. The differences will contribute to the overall scrappy look. All the buttons on this quilt appear to be different, but two of the buttons are actually identical—one was just sewn on upside down. You can get interesting effects by simply reversing some buttons.

Materials

Yardages are based on 42"-wide fabric.

¼ yard *each* of 7 assorted prints for blocks
1 yard of yellow print for blocks
⅝ yard of green plaid for outer border
⅝ yard of blue print for blocks
½ yard of purple-and-green striped print for blocks
⅜ yard of multicolored dot print for inner border
⅓ yard of multicolored plaid for blocks and inner-border cornerstones
⅝ yard of red print for binding
3¼ yards of fabric for backing
56" x 56" piece of batting
25 assorted-color buttons, 1" diameter

Cutting

All measurements include ¼"-wide seam allowances.

From the yellow print, cut:

- 4 strips, 4⅞" x 42"; crosscut into 26 squares, 4⅞" x 4⅞". Cut the squares in half once diagonally to yield 52 triangles.
- 2 strips, 5¼" x 42"; crosscut into 13 squares, 5¼" x 5¼". Cut the squares in half twice diagonally to yield 52 triangles.

From the blue print, cut:

- 3 strips, 3⅜" x 42"; crosscut into 24 squares, 3⅜" x 3⅜". Cut the squares in half once diagonally to yield 48 triangles.
- 2 strips, 3¾" x 42"; crosscut into 12 squares, 3¾" x 3¾". Cut the squares in half twice diagonally to yield 48 triangles.

From *each* of the 7 assorted prints, cut:

- 1 strip, 5¼" x 42"; crosscut into 2 squares, 5¼" x 5¼". Cut the squares in half twice diagonally to yield 8 triangles (56 total; 4 left over). From the remainder of 6 of the strips, cut 2 squares, 3¾" x 3¾"; cut the squares in half twice diagonally to yield 8 triangles (48 total).

From the purple-and-green striped print, cut:

- 7 strips, 2" x 42"; crosscut into 48 pieces, 2" x 5½"

From the multicolored plaid, cut:

- 3 strips, 2" x 42"; crosscut into 48 squares, 2" x 2"
- 1 strip, 2½" x 42"; crosscut into 4 squares, 2½" x 2½"

From the multicolored dot print, cut:

- 4 strips, 2½" x 40½"

From the green plaid, cut:

- 5 strips, 3¼" x 42"

From the red print, cut:

- 6 strips, 2¾" x 42"

Carrot Cookies

One summer, my grandmother's garden produced a wealth of carrots. What does one do with a bumper crop of this good-for-you produce? She made (and we ate) dozens of these wonderful cookies with a surprise ingredient!

Cookies

¾ cup shortening
¾ cup sugar
1 egg
1 cup cooked, mashed carrots
1 teaspoon vanilla
2 cups flour
2 teaspoons baking powder
½ teaspoon salt

Cream together the shortening, sugar, and egg. Add the carrots, vanilla, and dry ingredients. Drop by teaspoonfuls onto a greased cookie sheet. Bake at 350° for 8 to 10 minutes. Spread frosting (recipe follows) over cooled cookies. Makes 3 dozen cookies.

Frosting

2 tablespoons butter, softened
3 tablespoons orange juice
1 cup powdered sugar
¼ teaspoon grated orange peel

Combine all ingredients and beat until smooth.

Making the Blocks

Choose a different color for the pinwheel spinners of each block. The more variety you use, the scrappier your quilt will look.

1. To make block A, with right sides together, sew a yellow triangle cut from the 5¼" squares to each of four matching assorted-print triangles of the same size as shown to make triangle-square units. Press the seam allowances toward the assorted prints. Trim the extended corners.

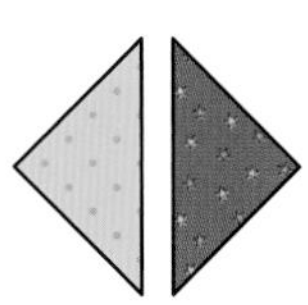

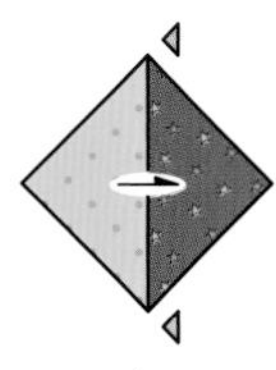

Make 4.

Note: The bias edges of the triangle-square units are on the outside, so handle the pieces carefully so as not to stretch them.

2. Join two of the triangle-square units as shown. Press the seam allowance as indicated. Make two.

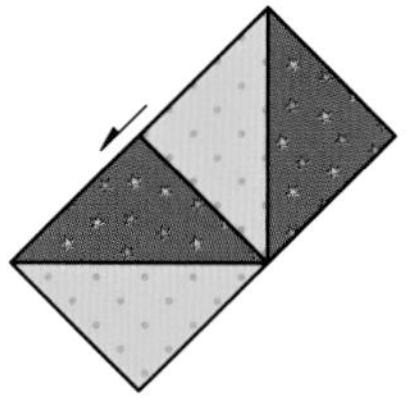

Make 2.

3. Sew the units together as shown. Before pressing, remove the vertical stitches in the seam allowances on both sides of each unit; then press the seam allowances in opposite directions. Where

the eight points meet in the middle, press the seams open so the unit makes a tiny pinwheel.

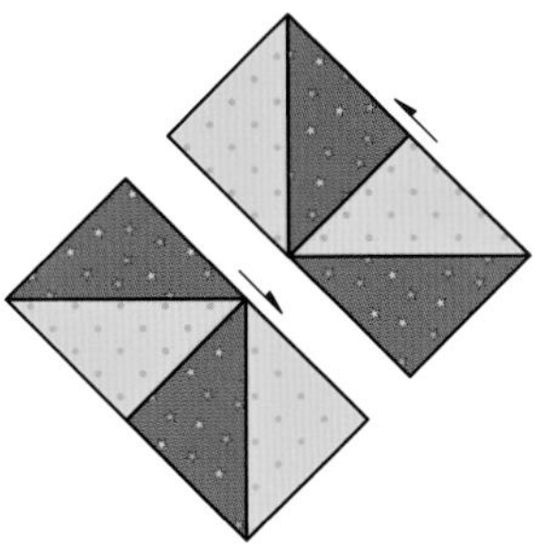

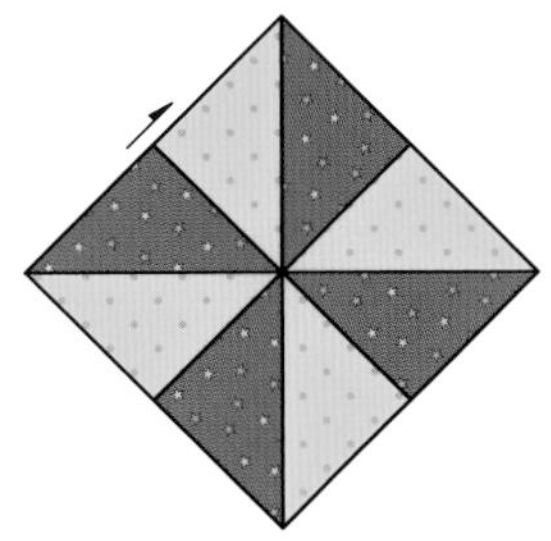

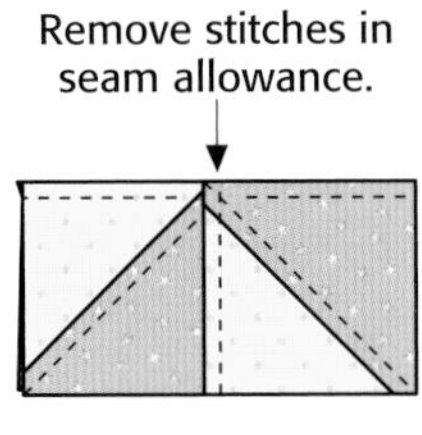

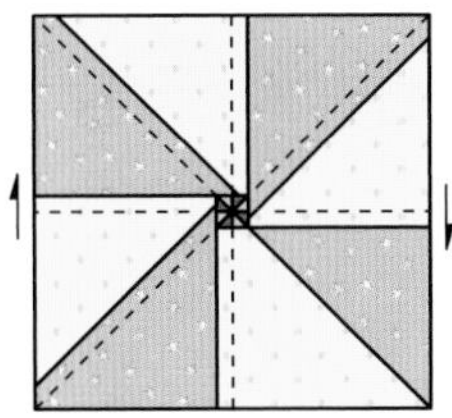

Press half of the seam up and half down.

4. Repeat steps 1–3 to make a total of 13 spinner units.
5. Sew a yellow triangle cut from the 4⅞" squares to opposite sides of each spinner unit. Press the seam allowances toward the corners. Sew a triangle to each of the remaining sides. Make 13 block A.

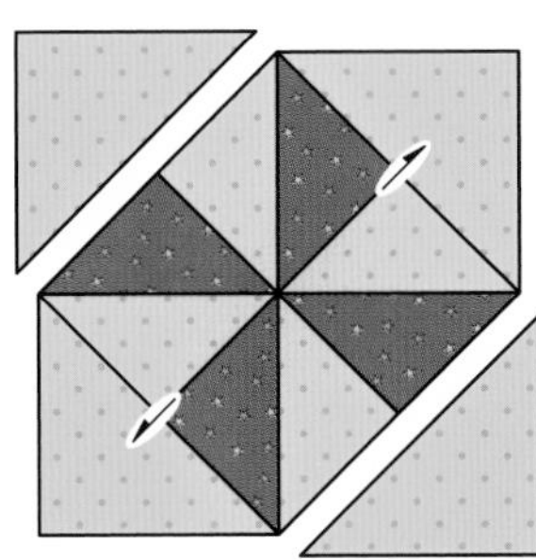

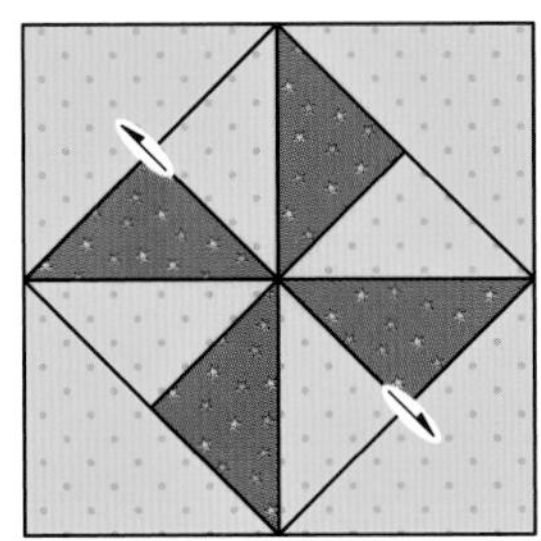

Block A.
Make 13.

6. To make block B, repeat step 1 with the blue and assorted-print triangles cut from the 3¾" squares.

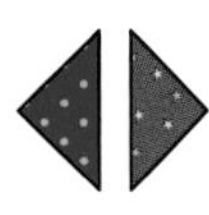

Make 12 sets of 4.

7. Repeat steps 2, 3, and 5 to join the units and add the blue triangles cut from the 3⅜" squares to the sides.

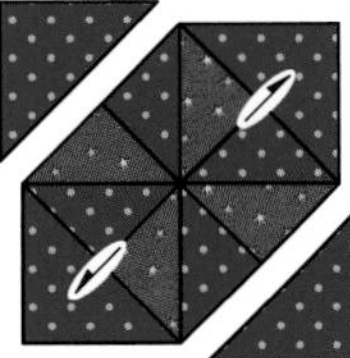

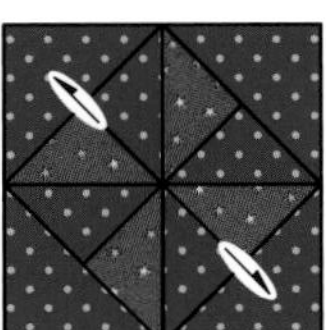

Make 12.

8. Sew a striped 2" x 5½" piece to opposite sides of each spinner unit as shown. Press the seam allowances toward the striped pieces.

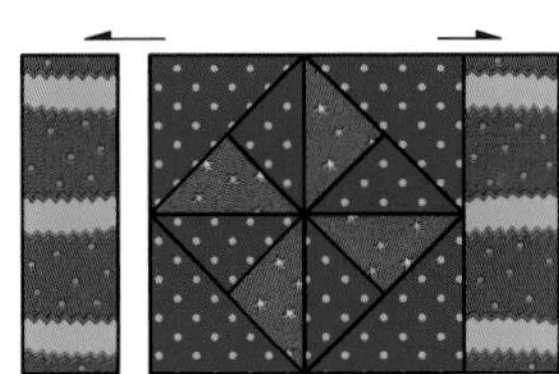

Make 12.

9. Sew a striped 2" x 5½" piece between two plaid 2" squares as shown. Press the seam allowances toward the stripe pieces. Repeat to make a total of 24 units.

Make 24.

10. Sew the units from step 10 to the spinner units as shown. Make 12 block B.

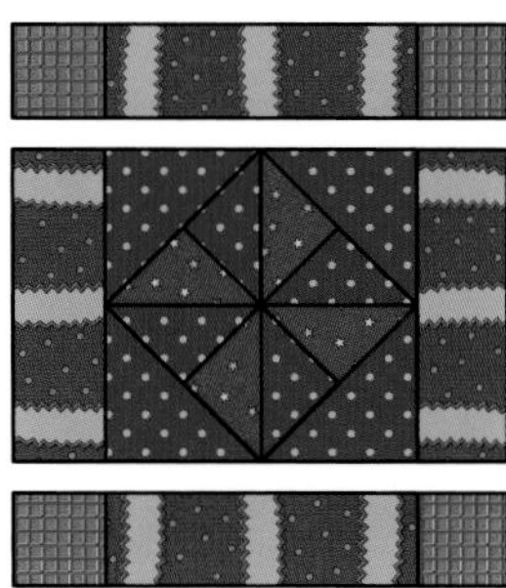

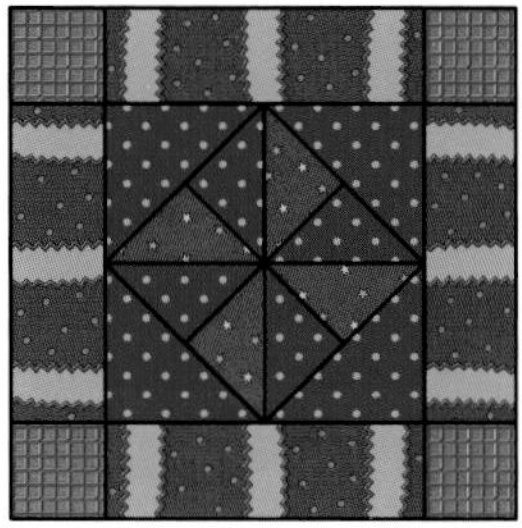

Block B.
Make 12.

Assembling the Quilt Top

1. Arrange the blocks into five horizontal rows as shown, alternating the position of blocks A and B in each row and from row to row as shown. Sew the blocks in each row together, pressing the seam allowances in opposite directions from row to row. Join the rows. Press the seam allowances in one direction.
2. Sew a multicolored dot strip to opposite sides of the quilt. Add the multicolored plaid 2½" squares to the ends of the remaining two multicolored dot strips. Sew these strips to the top and bottom of the quilt.
3. Refer to "Straight-Cut Borders" on page 89 to add the green plaid strips to the quilt for the outer border.

Finishing Your Quilt

Refer to "Quiltmaking Basics" on page 88 for specific instructions regarding each of the following steps.

1. Layer the quilt top with batting and backing; baste—unless you plan to take your quilt to a long-arm quilter.
2. Hand or machine quilt as desired.
3. Use the red 2¾"-wide strips to bind the quilt edges.
4. Embellish your quilt by sewing the buttons in the centers of the spinners as shown in the photo on page 52.

Play It Again

Skill level: *Beginner*

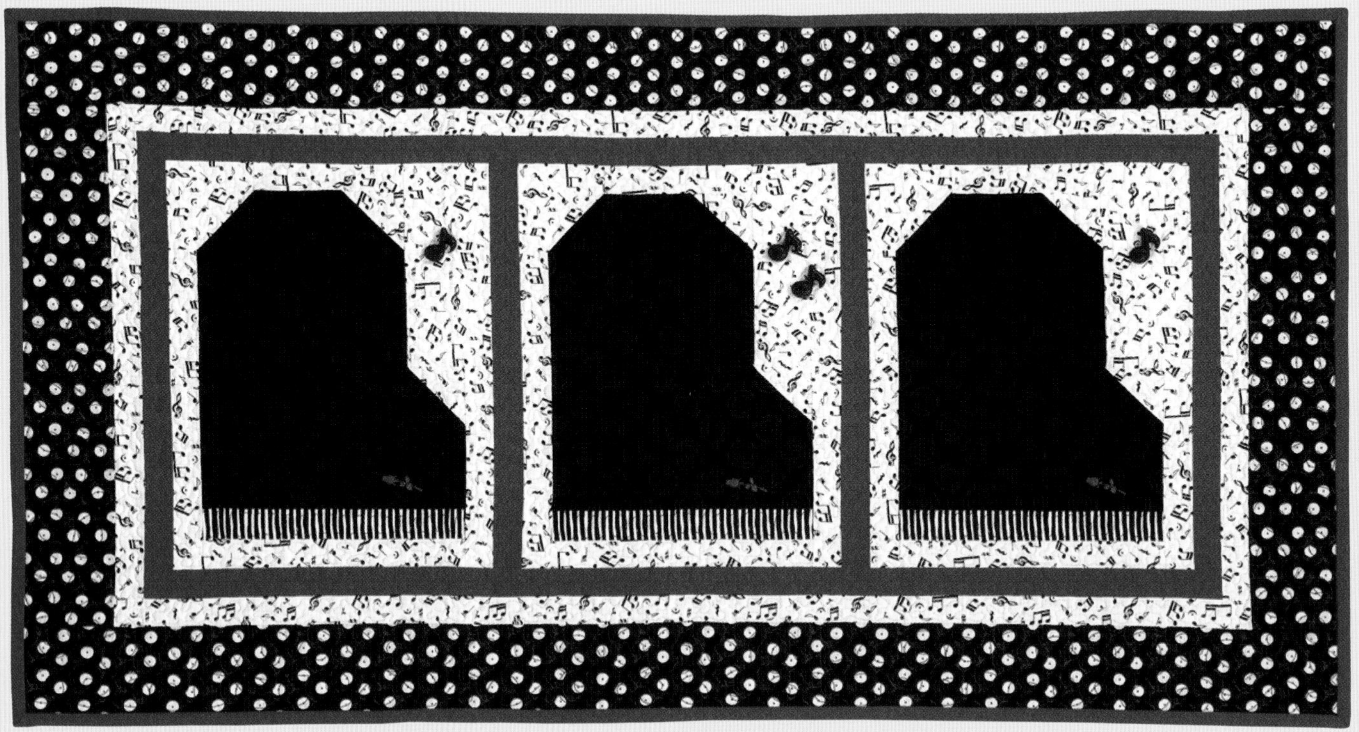

Finished quilt: 24½" x 45½" • **Finished block:** 11" x 14"

When we were growing up, the invention of the television brought lively entertainment right into our living room. At my grandmother's house, the **Lawrence Welk Show** *was a weekly musical interlude, and my grandparents would dance together around the living room to the sway of "champagne music."*
—Susan

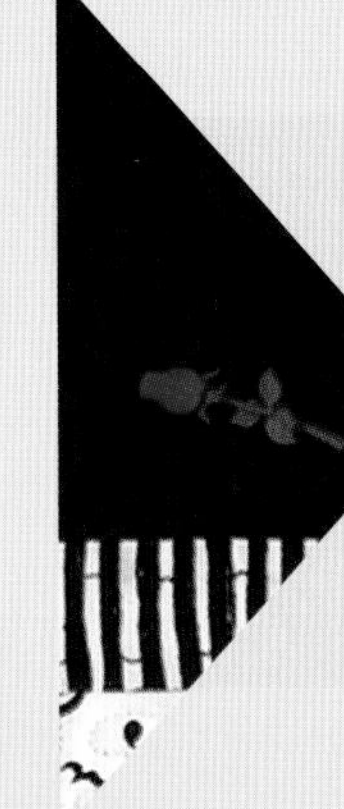

Button Box

The music notes are buttons, but the long-stemmed roses are findings, which aren't buttons but are easily secured to the quilt top with some stitches along the stem.

Materials

Yardages are based on 42"-wide fabric.

⅝ yard of white-with-black print for blocks and middle border

⅝ yard of red print for sashing, inner border, and binding

⅝ yard of black-with-white print for outer border

⅜ yard of black print for pianos

⅛ yard of black-and-white lengthwise stripe for keyboards

1⅝ yards of fabric for backing

30" x 51" piece of batting

4 black music-note buttons, 1⅛" long

3 long-stemmed rose findings, 1½" long

Cutting

All measurements include ¼"-wide seam allowances.

From the white-with-black print, cut:

- 1 strip, 3½" x 42"; crosscut into:
  - 3 pieces, 3½" x 4½"
  - 6 squares, 3½" x 3½"
- 6 squares, 2½" x 2½"
- 3 pieces, 1½" x 11½"
- 3 pieces, 1½" x 9½"
- 3 pieces, 1½" x 7½"
- 3 pieces, 1½" x 5½"
- 3 strips, 1½" x 42"

From the black print, cut:

- 3 pieces, 5½" x 9½"
- 3 pieces, 4½" x 7½"
- 3 pieces, 2½" x 5½"
- 3 squares, 2½" x 2½"

From the black-and-white stripe, cut:

- 3 pieces, 1½" x 9½"

From the red print, cut:

- 2 strips, 1½" x 37½"
- 4 pieces, 1½" x 14½"
- 4 strips, 2¾" x 42"

From the black-with-white print, cut:

- 4 strips, 3½" x 42"

Making the Blocks

1. Using a soft-lead pencil and a see-through ruler, draw a diagonal line from corner to corner on the wrong side of each white-with-black 2½" square and each black 2½" square.
2. With right sides together, position a white-with-black 2½" square on the upper right corner of each black 5½" x 9½" piece as shown. Stitch on the diagonal line. Trim ¼" from the stitching line; press the triangle and the seam allowance toward the corner.

Make 3.

3. Sew each stripe piece to a white-with-black 1½" x 9½" piece to make the keyboard sections. Press the seam allowances toward the stripe fabric.

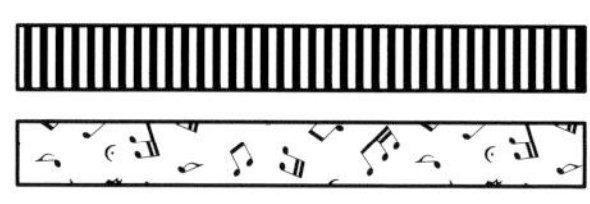

Make 3.

4. Sew a keyboard section from step 3 to each step 2 unit as shown. Press the seam allowance toward the step 2 unit.

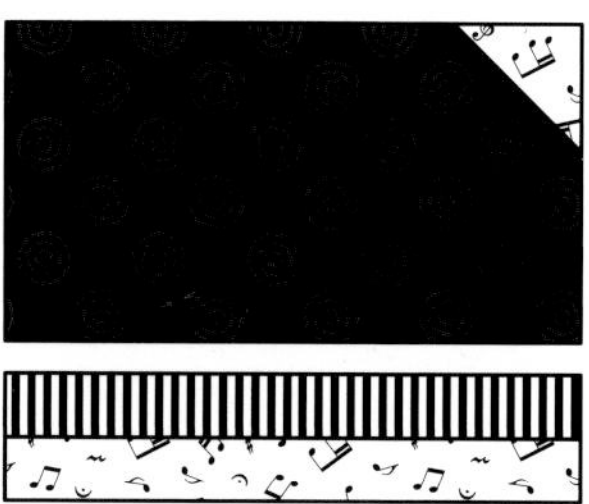

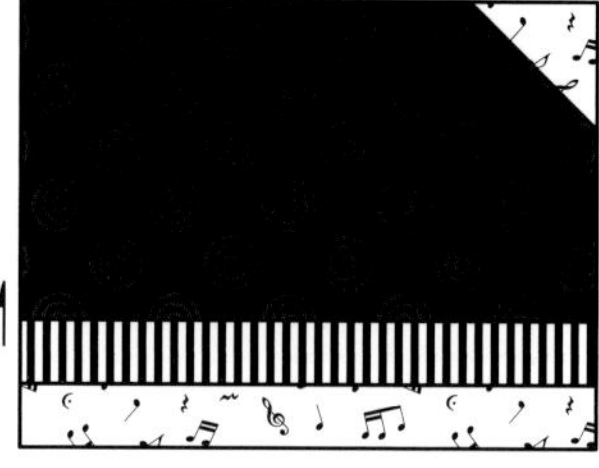

Make 3.

5. Sew a white-with-black 1½" x 7½" piece to the right side of each step 4 unit. Press the seam allowance toward the white piece.

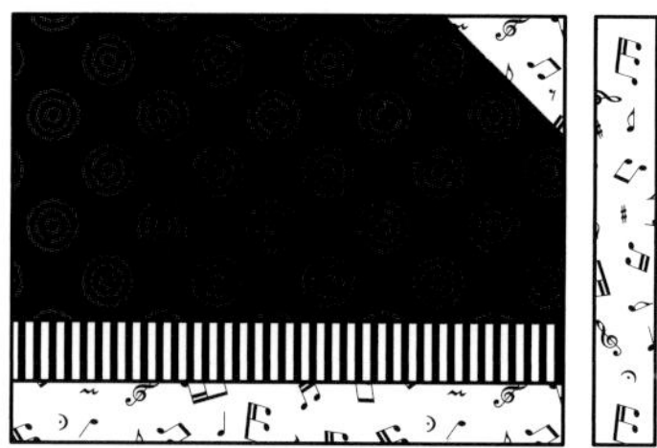

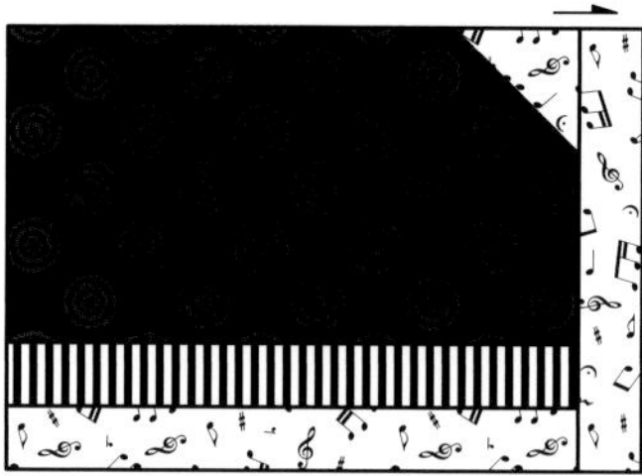

Make 3.

6. Sew each black 4½" x 7½" piece to a white-with-black 3½" x 4½" piece as shown. Press the seam allowances toward the black fabric. Join each unit to the top of each step 5 unit as shown. Press the seam allowances toward the top.

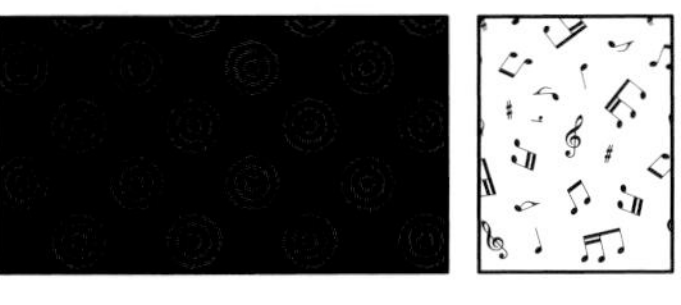

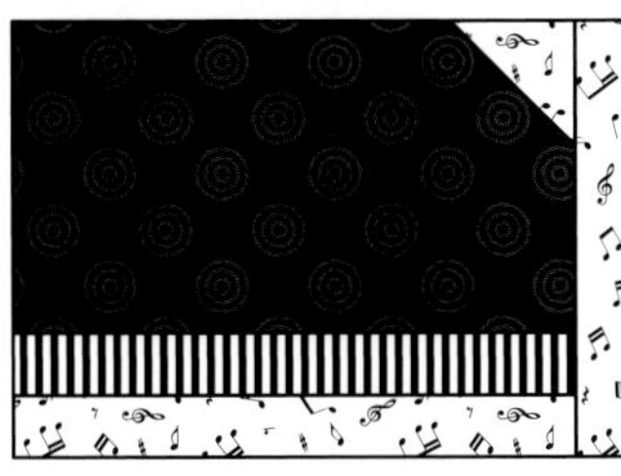

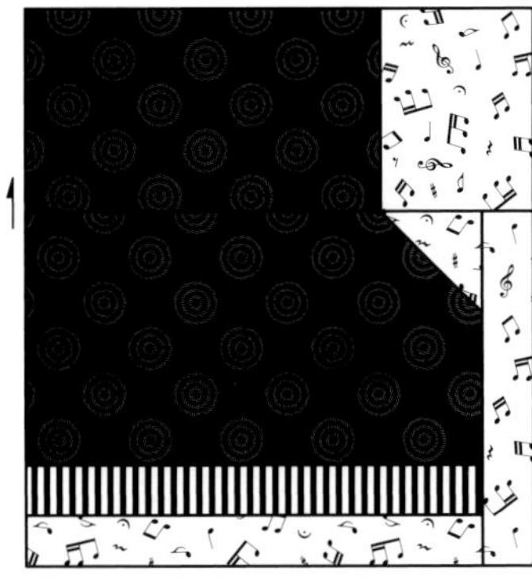

Make 3.

7. Sew a white-with-black 1½" x 11½" piece to the left side of each step 6 unit. Press the seam allowances toward the white piece.

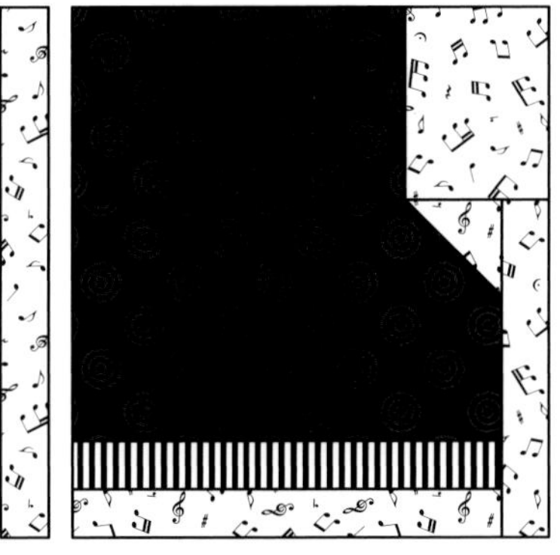

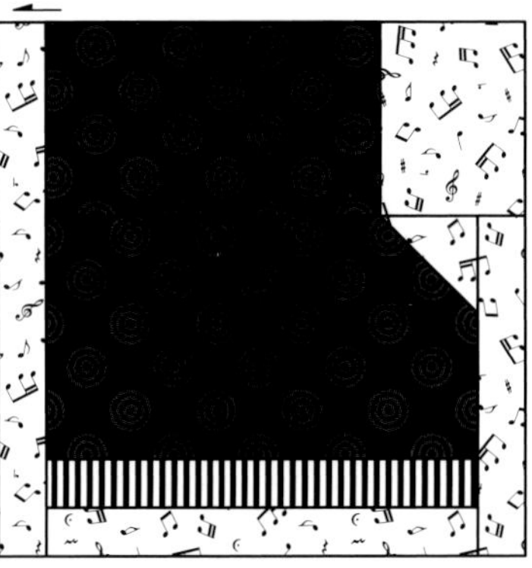

Make 3.

8. With right sides together, place a white-with-black 2½" square on one end of each black 2½" x 5½" piece as shown. Stitch, trim, and press as in step 2.

Make 3.

9. Sew a white-with-black 1½" x 5½" piece to the top of each step 8 unit as shown. Press the seam allowance toward the white piece.

Make 3.

10. Place a black 2½" square on the lower right corner of each white-with-black 3½" square as shown. Stitch, trim, and press as in step 2.

Make 3.

11. Sew each unit from step 9 between a step 10 unit and a white-with-black 3½" square as shown. Press the seam allowances as indicated.

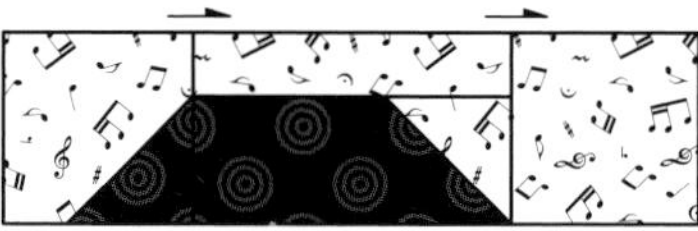

Make 3.

12. Complete the Piano blocks by joining each step 11 unit to the top of a step 7 unit. Press the seam allowances toward the step 7 units.

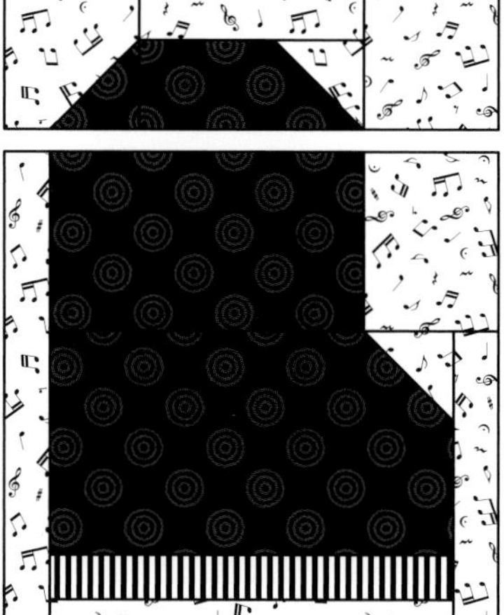
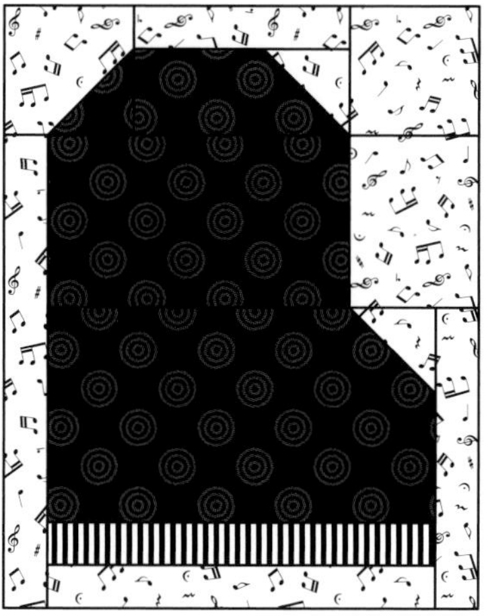

Make 3.

Assembling the Quilt Top

1. Sew the blocks between the red 1½" x 14½" pieces as shown. Press the seam allowances toward the red. Sew the red 1½" x 37½" strips to the top and bottom. Press the seam allowances toward the red.

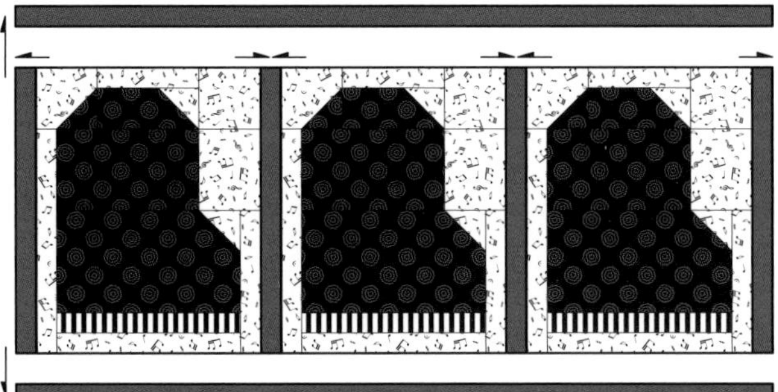

2. Refer to "Straight-Cut Borders" on page 89 to add the white-with-black 1½"-wide strips to the quilt for the inner border, and the black-with-white 3½"-wide strips for the outer border. Press all the seam allowances away from the quilt center.

Finishing Your Quilt

Refer to "Quiltmaking Basics" on page 88 for specific instructions regarding each of the following steps.

1. Layer the quilt top, batting, and backing; baste—unless you plan to take your quilt to a long-arm quilter.
2. Hand or machine quilt as desired.
3. Use the red 2¾"-wide strips to bind the quilt edges.
4. Embellish the quilt blocks with the buttons and findings as desired, or refer to the photo on page 58 for placement.
5. Sew a hanging sleeve to the back of the quilt if desired.

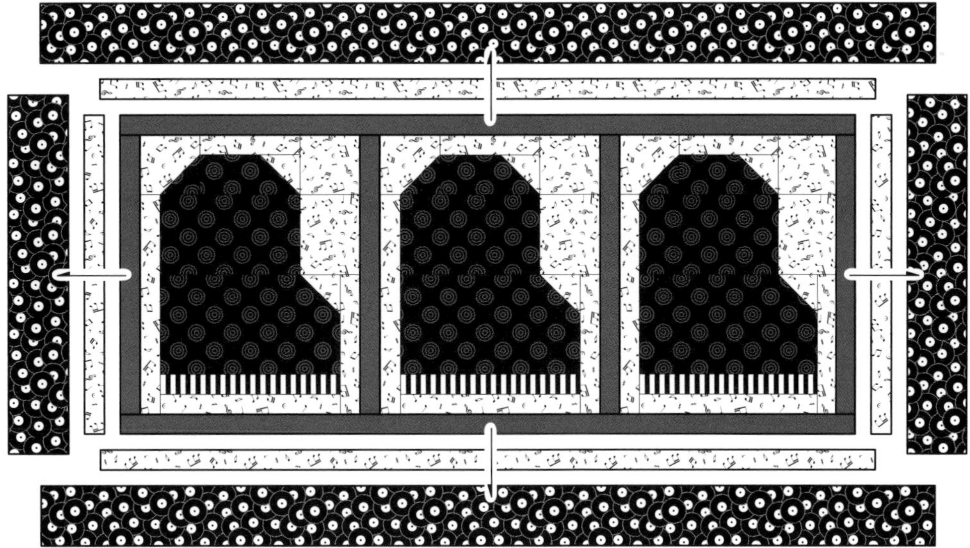

Flower Frenzy

Skill level: *Confident beginner*

Finished quilt: 33½" x 33½" • **Finished block:** 9" x 9"

Our grandmother, who preferred we call her Lucille, sewed draperies for homes that our grandfather built. Her sewing room was cluttered with swatch books and scraps of colorful chintz—yellow was always her personal color preference. This quilt is a tribute to her, for helping me make my first quilt from drapery swatches and for sharing her love of beautiful fabrics with me. Thank you, Lucille.
—Loraine

Button Box

The buttons in the corners of this quilt are vintage Bakelite buttons I found at a flea market. The flower centers were the perfect showcase for contemporary navy blue buttons.

Materials

Yardages are based on 42"-wide fabric.

¾ yard of dark blue print for block A and binding

⅝ yard of yellow print for blocks

⅝ yard of medium blue print for blocks and border cornerstones

⅝ yard of blue check print for border and large flowers

¼ yard of light green print for block B

¼ yard of dark green print for leaves

⅛ yard of medium green print for leaves

⅛ yard of yellow check print for small flowers

1⅛ yards of fabric for backing

Batting: 40" x 40" piece for quilt; 36" x 36" piece for flowers and leaves

4 navy blue buttons, 1" diameter

4 light blue buttons, ¾" diameter

Cutting

All measurements include ¼"-wide seam allowances.

To cut the flower and leaf shapes, trace patterns A–D on page 69 onto paper and cut out the shapes. Place two pieces of the appropriate fabric, right sides together, on top of a piece of batting. Pin the appropriate pattern piece to this fabric-and-batting "sandwich" and cut through all of the layers. Remove the pattern and pin the pieces together so the layers stay intact once they are cut. Repeat to make the required amount of sandwiches for each pattern.

From the dark blue print, cut:

- 2 strips, 3½" x 42"; crosscut into 20 squares, 3½" x 3½"
- 2 strips, 2" x 42"
- 4 strips, 2¾" x 42"

From the medium blue print, cut:

- 2 strips, 3½" x 42"; crosscut into 16 squares, 3½" x 3½"
- 5 strips, 2" x 42"; crosscut 1 strip into 20 squares, 2" x 2"

From the yellow print, cut:
- 1 strip, 3½" x 42"; crosscut into 9 squares, 3½" x 3½"
- 6 strips, 2" x 42"; crosscut into 108 squares, 2" x 2"

From the light green print, cut:
- 3 strips, 2" x 42"; crosscut 1 strip into 16 squares, 2" x 2"

From the blue check print, cut:
- 4 strips, 3½" x 42"; crosscut into 4 pieces, 3½" x 27½"
- 4 large flower sandwiches, using pattern A

From the yellow check print, cut:
- 4 small flower sandwiches, using pattern B

From the dark green print, cut:
- 12 large leaf sandwiches, using pattern C

From the medium green print, cut:
- 16 small leaf sandwiches, using pattern D

Making the Blocks

1. Using a soft-lead pencil and a see-through ruler, draw a diagonal line from corner to corner on the wrong side of each 2" square.
2. To make block A, sew a dark blue 2"-wide strip and a medium blue 2"-wide strip together as shown to make a strip set. Press the seam allowance toward the dark blue. Make two strip sets. Cut the strip sets into 20 segments, 3½" wide.

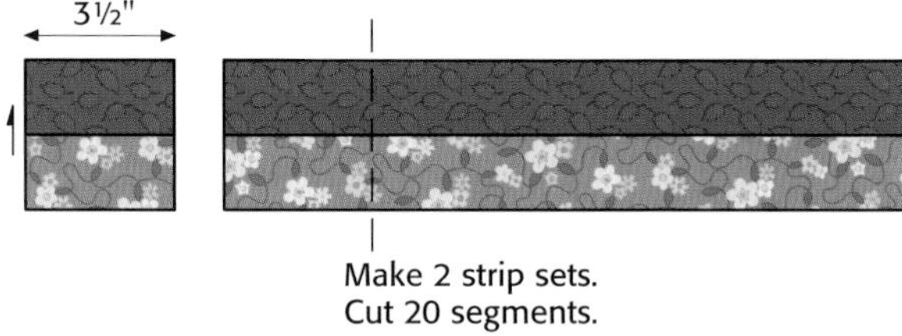

Make 2 strip sets.
Cut 20 segments.

3. With right sides together, position a medium blue 2" square on one corner of a dark blue 3½" square as shown. Place a yellow 2" square on the opposite corner as shown. Stitch on the diagonal lines. Trim ¼" from the stitching lines; press the triangles and the seam allowances toward the corners. Position a yellow 2" square on each of the opposite corners as shown. Stitch, trim, and press as before. Repeat to make a total of 20 units.

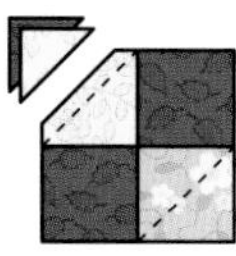
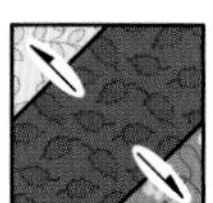
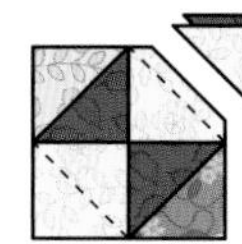
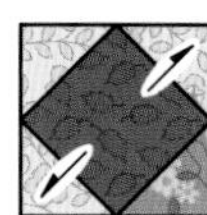

Make 20.

4. Sew a step 2 unit between two step 3 units as shown. Press the seam allowances toward the step 2 units. Repeat to make a total of 10 rows.

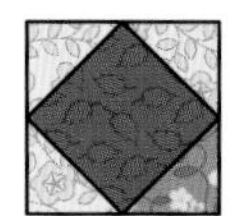
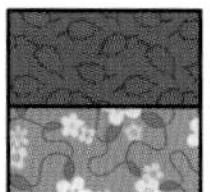
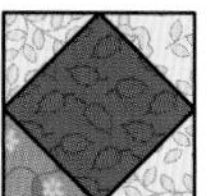

Make 10.

5. Sew a yellow 3½" square between two step 2 units as shown. Press the seam allowance toward the step 2 units. Repeat to make a total of five rows.

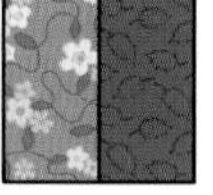
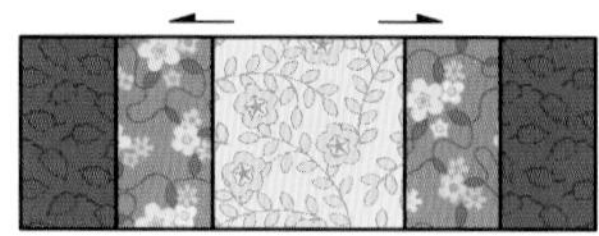

Make 5.

6. Arrange the steps 4 and 5 rows as shown. Sew the rows together to complete block A. Press the seam allowances toward the center row. Repeat to make a total of five blocks.

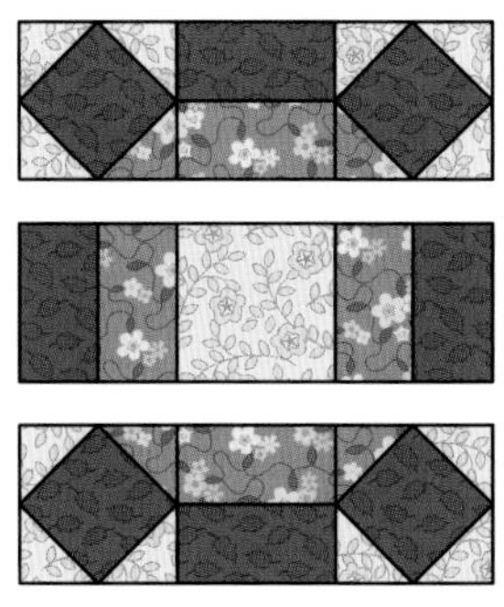

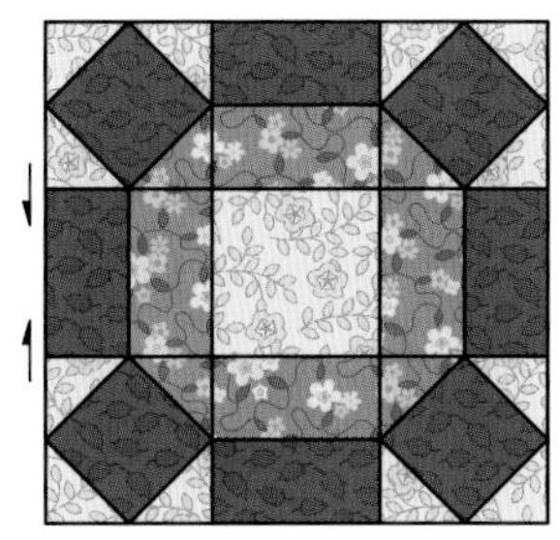

Block A.
Make 5.

7. To make block B, repeat step 2 to make two strip sets from the medium blue and light green 2"-wide strips. Crosscut the strip sets into 16 segments, 3½" wide.

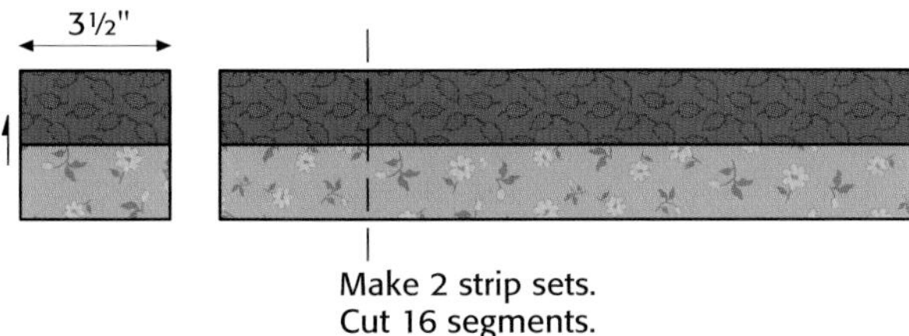

Make 2 strip sets.
Cut 16 segments.

8. Repeat step 3 with the medium blue 3½" squares and the yellow and light green 2" squares to make 16 units as shown.

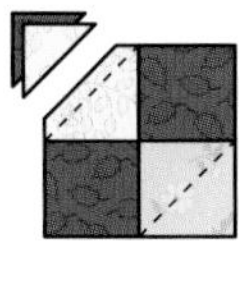

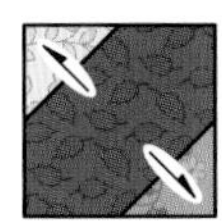

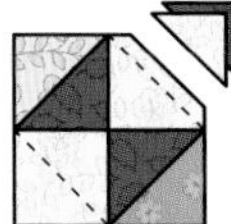

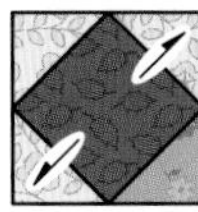

Make 16.

9. Sew a step 7 unit between two step 8 units as shown. Press the seam allowances toward the step 7 unit. Repeat to make a total of eight rows.

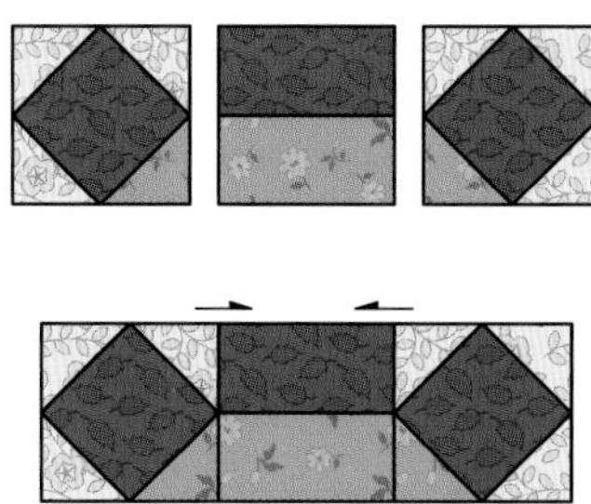

Make 8.

10. Sew a yellow 3½" square between two step 7 units. Press the seam allowances toward the step 7 units. Repeat to make a total of four rows.

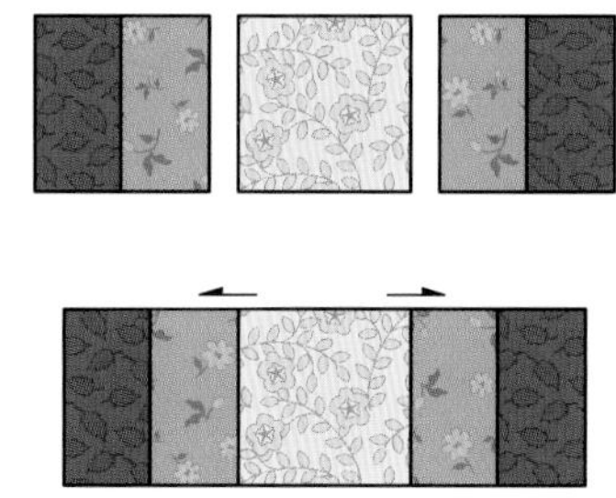

Make 4.

11. Arrange the steps 9 and 10 rows as shown. Sew the rows together to complete block B. Press the seam allowances away from the center row. Repeat to make a total of four blocks.

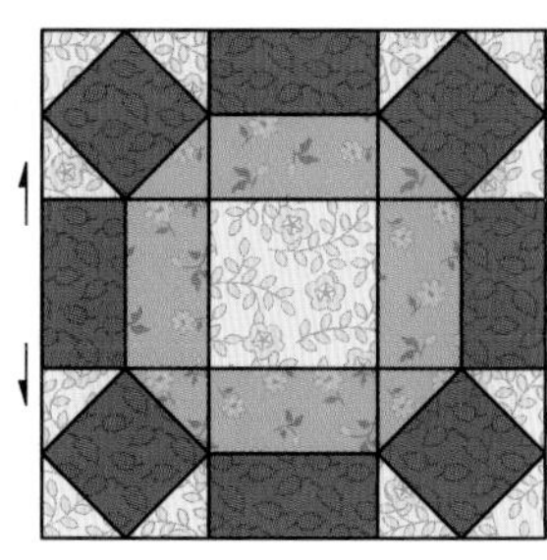

Block B.
Make 4.

Assembling the Quilt Top

1. Arrange the blocks into three horizontal rows as shown, alternating the position of blocks A and B in each row and from row to row as shown. Sew the blocks in each row together, pressing the seam allowances in opposite directions from row to row. Join the rows. Press the seam allowances in one direction.
2. Sew a blue check 3½" x 27½" piece to opposite sides of the quilt. Press the seam allowance toward the borders. Sew a medium blue 3½" square to the ends of the remaining two blue check pieces. Add these borders to the top and bottom of the quilt. Press the seam allowances toward the borders.

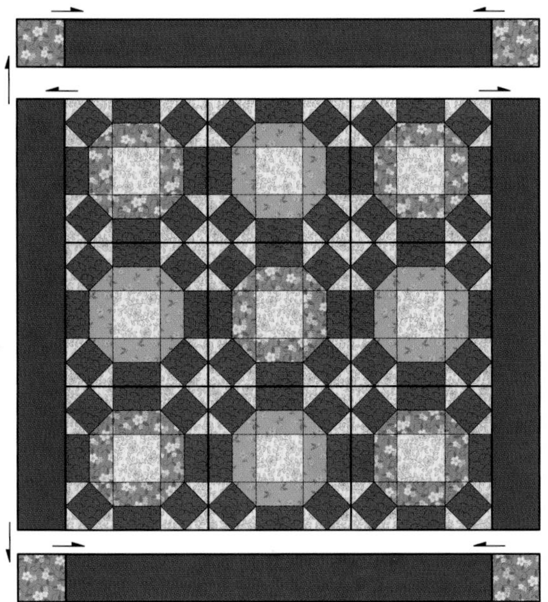

Finishing Your Quilt

Refer to "Quiltmaking Basics" on page 88 for specific instructions regarding each of the following steps.

1. Layer the quilt top with batting and backing; baste—unless you plan to take your quilt to a long-arm quilter.
2. Hand or machine quilt as desired.
3. Use the dark blue 2¾"-wide strips to bind the quilt edges.
4. With the batting side down, sew around each flower and leaf sandwich, using a ¼" seam allowance. Clip the seams of the flower shapes as shown and trim the points of the leaf shapes. Cut a 1"-long slit through the center of the top layer of fabric and turn the pieces to the right side; press.

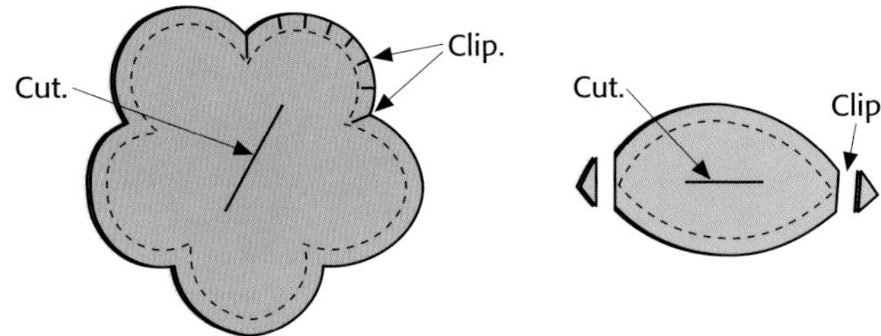

5. Arrange the flower and leaf shapes on the quilt top as shown in the photo on page 64. Secure them to the quilt by sewing through all layers along the quilting lines, indicated on the patterns.

6. Attach the navy blue buttons to the center of each flower, and the light blue buttons to the center of each border cornerstone.
7. Sew a hanging sleeve to the back of the quilt if desired.

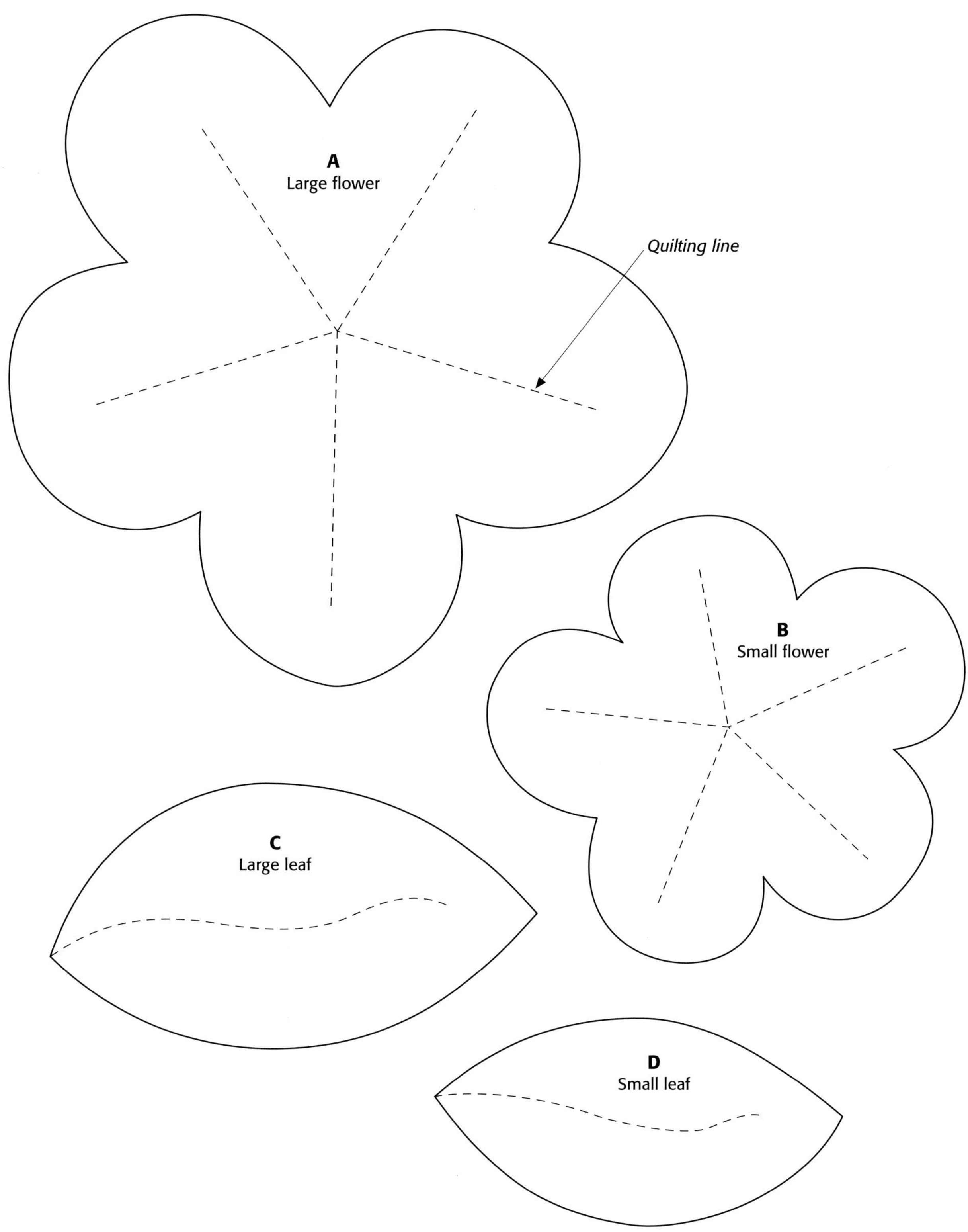
A
Large flower
Quilting line
B
Small flower
C
Large leaf
D
Small leaf

Cherries Jubilee

Skill level: *Beginner*

Finished quilt: 50½" x 50½" • **Finished block:** 8" x 8"

The popular 1940s tablecloth, brightly printed with images of fruit, is updated with reproduction fabrics in this cheery cherry quilt for the kitchen, dining room, or backyard picnic table.
—Susan

Button Box

The cherry buttons in the outer-border cornerstones were the inspiration for this quilt. I found them, bought them, and then decided what to do with them. At first, I thought the quilt was complete with the cherries at the corners, but then I decided that I wanted more cherries throughout the quilt and added one or two red buttons to each block.

Materials

Yardages are based on 42"-wide fabric.

2½ yards of red print for blocks, inner border, pieced outer border, and binding

1⅞ yards of blue-with-white dots print for blocks and pieced outer border

⅝ yard of white-with-blue dots print for blocks

⅜ yard of blue-with-red print for blocks

3¼ yards of fabric for backing

56" x 56" piece of batting

35 red buttons, ⅝" diameter

4 sets of cherry buttons (JHB 28201) for outer-border cornerstones

Cutting

All measurements include ¼"-wide seam allowances.

From the blue-with-white dots print, cut:

- 12 strips, 4½" x 42"; crosscut into:
  - 100 rectangles, 2½" x 4½"
  - 28 pieces, 4½" x 6½"
  - 4 squares, 4½" x 4½"
- 3 strips, 2½" x 42"; crosscut into 48 squares, 2½" x 2½"

From the white-with-blue dots print, cut:

- 4 strips, 4½" x 42"; crosscut into 25 squares, 4½" x 4½"

From the red print, cut:

- 10 strips, 2½" x 42"; crosscut into 152 squares, 2½" x 2½"
- 7 strips, 4½" x 42"; crosscut into 56 squares, 4½" x 4½"
- 5 strips, 1½" x 42"
- 6 strips, 2¾" x 42"

From the blue-with-red print, cut:

- 4 strips, 2½" x 42"; crosscut into 52 squares, 2½" x 2½"

Mile-High Strawberry Pie

When we were children, this was a favorite party treat. Our grandmother delighted us with it time after time, and often we helped as she turned the ingredients into a miraculous pink cloud. It's the perfect ending for a summer meal.

8-ounce package of frozen strawberries, thawed

¾ cup sugar

Dash salt

1 tablespoon bottled lemon juice

2 unbeaten egg whites

½ pint whipping cream

2 baked piecrusts or graham cracker-crumb pie shells, 9"

Combine strawberries, sugar, salt, lemon juice, and egg whites in a mixing bowl. Beat on low speed 5 minutes. Beat on medium speed 5 minutes. Beat on high speed 5 minutes. In a separate bowl, whip the cream and fold into the mixture. Turn the mixture into the piecrusts. Freeze for 6 hours. Serve frozen. Makes two 9" pies.

Making the Blocks

1. Using a soft-lead pencil and a see-through ruler, draw a diagonal line from corner to corner on the wrong side of each blue-with-white dots 2½" square, each red 4½" square, and 104 of the red 2½" squares.
2. To make block A, with right sides together, position a blue-with-white dots 2½" square on opposite corners of a white-with-blue dots square as shown. Stitch on the diagonal lines. Trim ¼" from the stitching lines; press the triangles and the seam allowances toward the corners. Position a blue-with-white dots 2½" square on the remaining two corners as shown. Stitch, trim, and press as before. Repeat to make a total of 12 units.

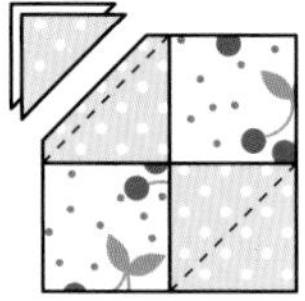
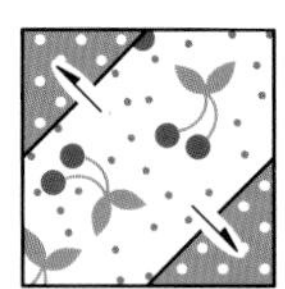
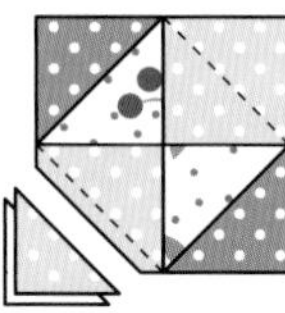
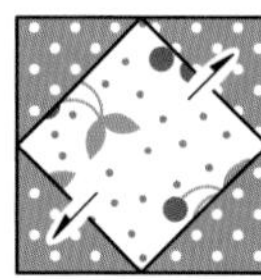

Make 12.

3. Arrange four red 2½" squares, four blue-with-white dots 2½" x 4½" rectangles, and one step 2 unit into three horizontal rows as shown. Sew the pieces in each row together. Press the seam allowances as indicated. Sew each row together. Press the seam allowances as indicated. Repeat to make a total of 12 block A.

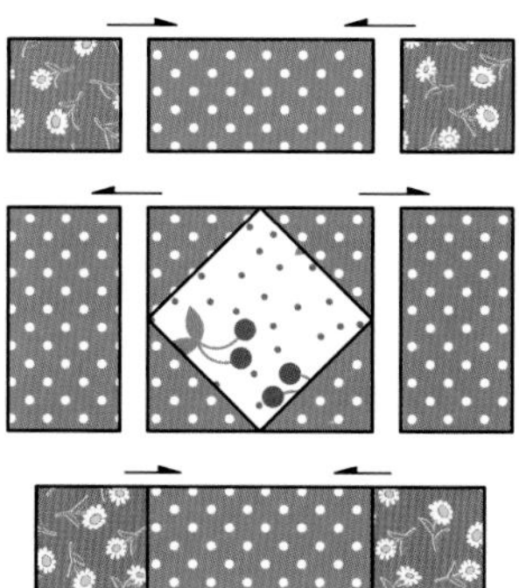
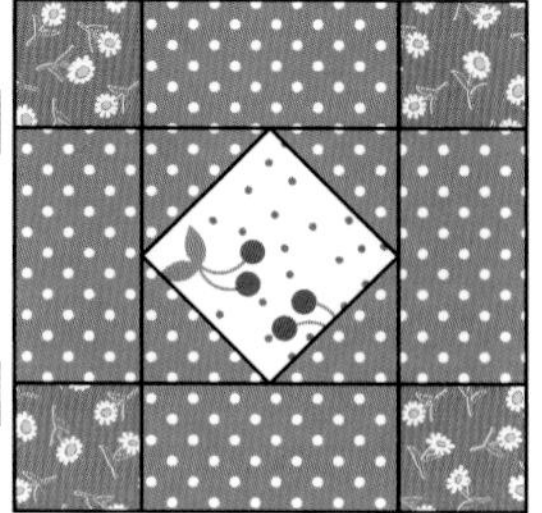

Block A.
Make 12.

4. To make block B, place a red 2½" square on one end of a blue-with-white dots 2½" x 4½" rectangle, right sides together, as shown. Stitch on the diagonal line. Trim ¼" from the stitching line; press the triangle and the seam allowance toward the corner. Position another red 2½" square on the opposite end of the piece as shown. Stitch, trim, and press as before. Repeat to make a total of 52 units.

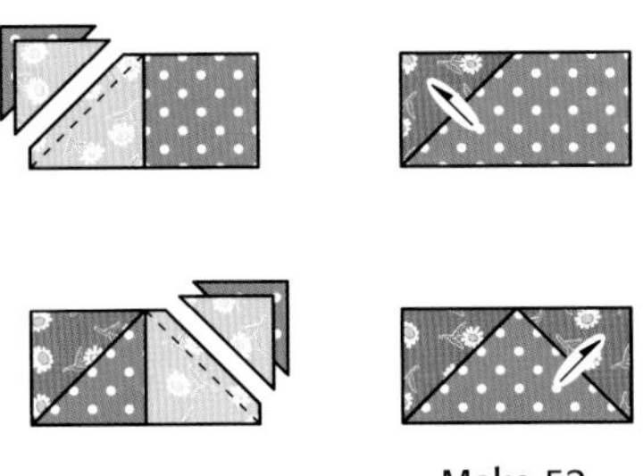

Make 52.

5. Arrange four blue-with-red squares, four step 4 units, and one white-with-blue dots square into three horizontal rows as shown. Stitch the pieces in each row together. Press the seam allowances as indicated. Sew the rows together. Press the seam allowances as indicated. Repeat to make a total of 13 block B.

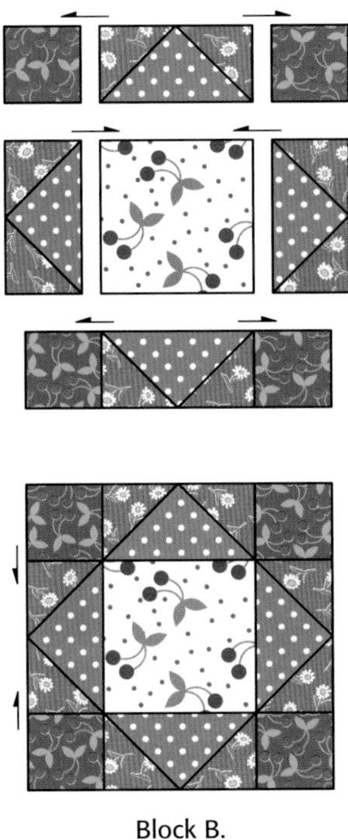

Block B.
Make 13.

Assembling the Quilt Top

1. Arrange the blocks into five horizontal rows as shown, alternating the position of blocks A and B in each row and from row to row as shown. Sew the blocks in each row together, pressing the seam allowances in opposite directions from row to row. Join the rows. Press the seam allowances in one direction.

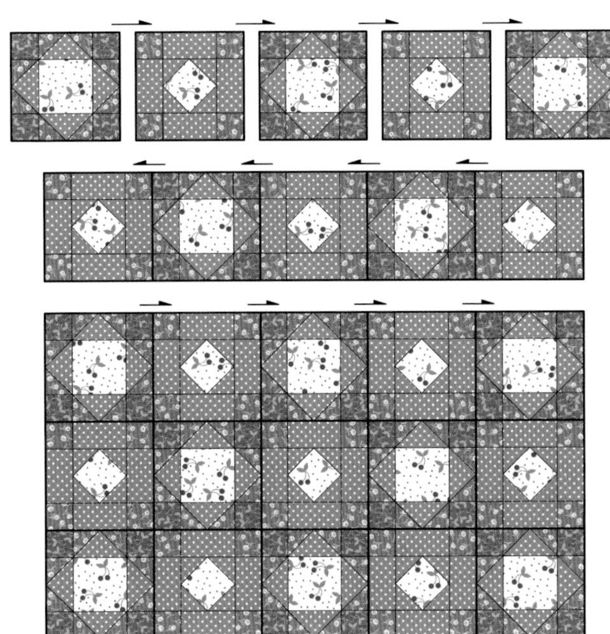

2. Refer to "Straight-Cut Borders" on page 89 to add the red 1½"-wide strips to the quilt top for the inner border. Press the seam allowances toward the border.

3. To make the pieced border, place a red 4½" square on one end of a blue-with-white dots 4½" x 6½" piece as shown. Stitch on the diagonal line. Trim ¼" from the stitching line and press the seam allowance toward the corner. Place another red 4½" square on the opposite end of the piece as shown. Stitch, trim, and press as before. Repeat to make a total of 28 units.

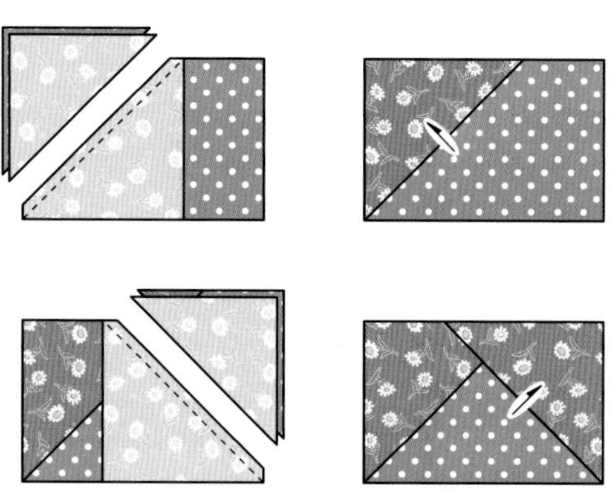

Make 28.

4. Join seven step 3 units to make an outer-border row. Press the seam allowances in one direction. Repeat to make a total of four rows.

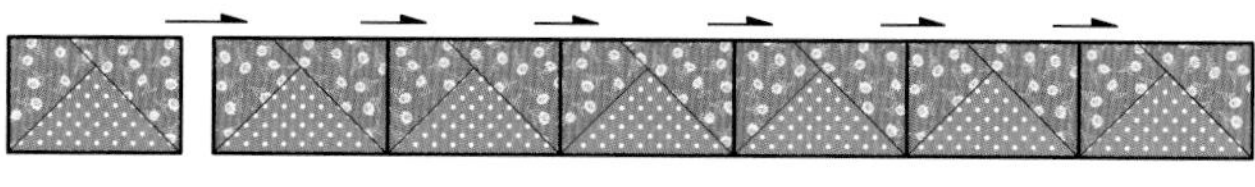

Make 4.

5. Sew an outer-border row to opposite sides of the quilt top as shown. Press the seam allowances toward the inner border. Add a blue-with-white dots 4½" square to each end of the remaining two rows and sew the rows to the top and bottom of the quilt. Press the seam allowances toward the inner border.

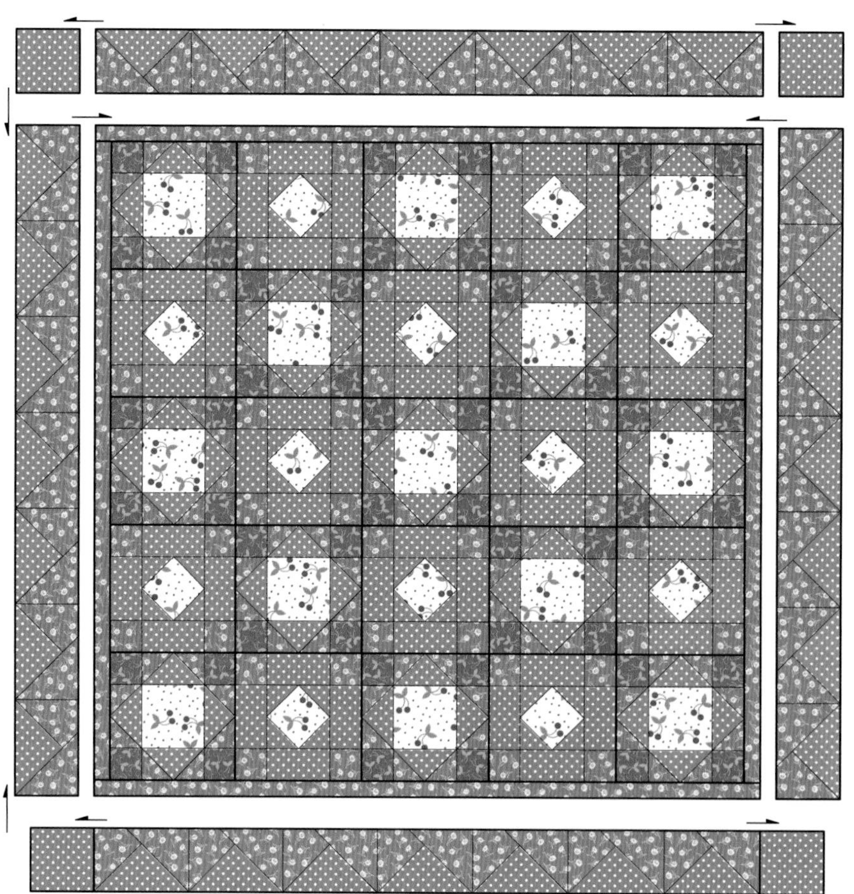

Finishing Your Quilt

Refer to "Quiltmaking Basics" on page 88 for specific instructions regarding each of the following steps.

1. Layer the quilt top, batting, and backing; baste—unless you plan to take your quilt to a long-arm quilter.
2. Hand or machine quilt as desired.
3. Use the red 2¾"-wide strips to bind the quilt edges.
4. Embellish the quilt with the buttons as shown in the photo on page 70, or create your own arrangement.
5. Sew a hanging sleeve to the back of the quilt if desired.

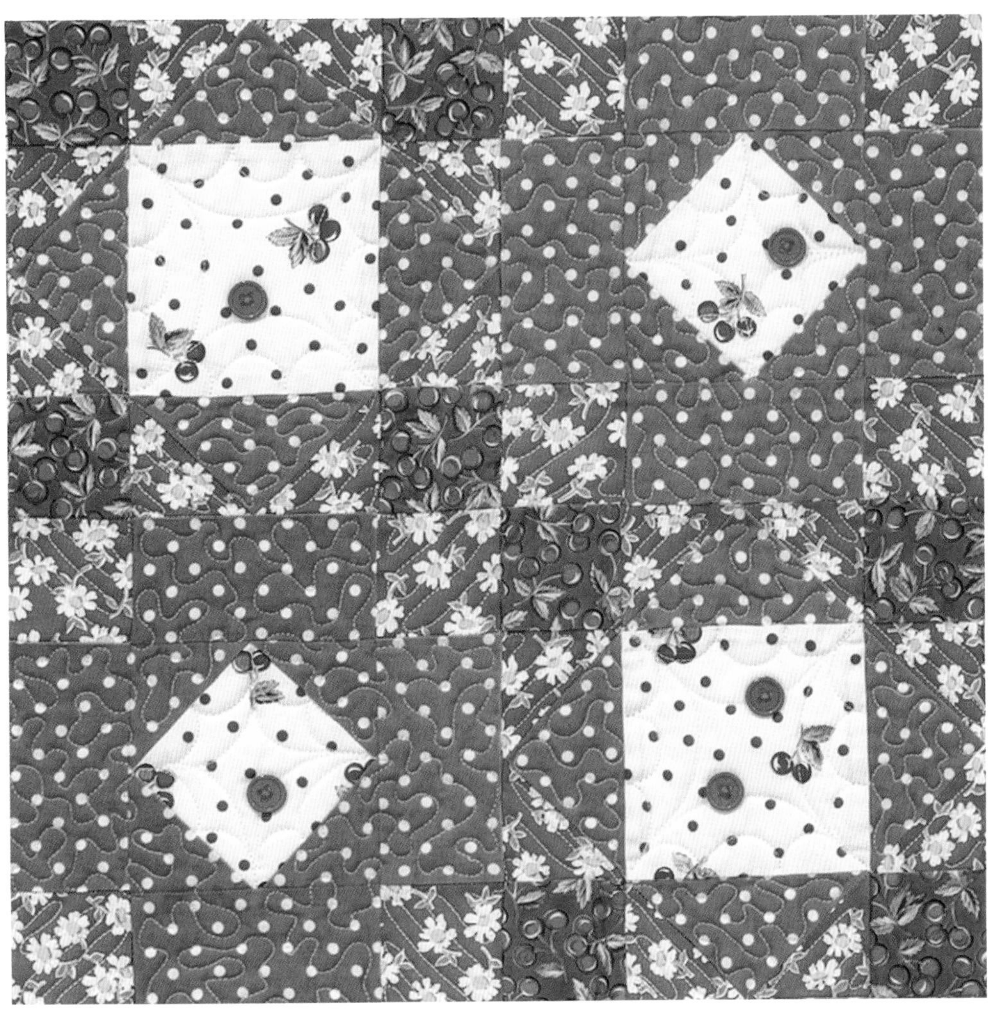

Under the Stars

Skill level: *Intermediate*

Finished quilt: 69½" x 69½" • **Finished block:** 17" x 17"

Staying at my grandparents' home always meant sleeping under one of my grandmother's quilts. The colorful fabrics and variety of quilt blocks were as entertaining to me as a picture book. This Feathered Star quilt is my version of one of the quilts I remember.
—Loraine

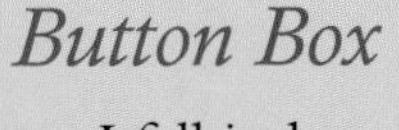

Button Box

I fell in love with these vintage, ruby-colored glass buttons and decided that using all 72 of them would definitely add some sparkle to the feathered stars!

Materials

Yardages are based on 42"-wide fabric.

2¼ yards of white print for blocks

2 yards of lengthwise-stripe floral print with stripes that are approximately but no wider than 2¾" for sashing

1⅞ yards of black print for blocks and binding

1⅜ yards of diagonally printed plaid for blocks and border

1⅛ yards of floral print for blocks

⅝ yard of red print for blocks

¼ yard of black-and-white floral print for sashing cornerstones

5 yards of fabric for backing

76" x 76" piece of batting

72 red buttons, ¾" diameter

Template plastic

Storing Your Pieces

Don't be afraid—as many pieces as this Feathered Star block has, it's very forgiving. As you cut the pieces for the blocks, you'll find it helpful to place them in labeled, reclosable storage bags until you're ready to use them.

Cutting

All measurements include ¼"-wide seam allowances.

Before you begin cutting, trace patterns A and B on page 83 onto template plastic and cut them out. Use the templates to cut the indicated pieces. To fussy cut the floral stripes, use a see-through acrylic ruler as a cutting guide. Cut the stripes the required width so that the floral motif is centered in the strip you want to cut.

From the white print, cut:

- 6 strips, 5½" x 42"; crosscut into 36 squares, 5½" x 5½"
- 3 strips, 5⅞" x 42"; crosscut into 18 squares, 5⅞" x 5⅞". Cut the squares once diagonally to yield 36 triangles.
- 10 strips, 2" x 42"

From the black print, cut:

- 2 strips, 2¼" x 42"; crosscut into 18 squares, 2¼" x 2¼". Cut the squares once diagonally to yield 36 triangles.
- 14 strips, 2" x 42"; crosscut 4 of the strips into 72 squares, 2" x 2". Cut the squares once diagonally to yield 144 triangles.
- 2 strips, 1⅞" x 42"; crosscut into 36 squares, 1⅞" x 1⅞"
- 8 strips, 2¾" x 42"

From the plaid, cut:

- 2 strips, 5¼" x 42"; crosscut into 9 squares, 5¼" x 5¼"
- 8 strips, 4" x 42"

From the red print, cut:

- 10 strips, 1¾" x 42". From the strips, cut 72 template A pieces.

From the floral print, cut:

- 10 strips, 3¼" x 42". From the strips, cut 72 template B pieces.

From the black-and-white floral print, cut:

- 2 strips, 3¼" x 42"; crosscut into 16 squares, 3¼" x 3¼"

From the stripe print, fussy cut:

- 8 stripe strips, 3¼" x 63", along the lengthwise grain; crosscut into 24 pieces, 3¼" x 17½"

What's Old Is New Again

My grandmother was always looking for ways to improve things that were old and well used. I remember that one summer she covered every pieced quilt she had with new fabric and tied each one with yarn. Thus, her beautiful old quilts became new comforters.

Making the Blocks

1. Place each white 2"-wide strip right sides together with a black 2"-wide strip, aligning the edges. On the wrong side of the white strips, use a soft-lead pencil and a see-through ruler to lightly mark the strips into as many 2" squares as possible. Mark a total of 180 squares. (If you can mark 20 squares on each strip, then you'll need only nine pairs.) Draw a diagonal line from corner to corner on each marked square, alternating the direction of the lines as shown. Beginning on one end of each strip, sew a scant ¼" from one side of the marked lines in one continuous seam. Then turn back and sew a scant ¼" seam on the other side of the marked lines. Cut the squares apart on the marked 2"-square lines and then cut the squares in half on the diagonal lines to make 360 triangle-square units. Press the seam allowances toward the black fabric. Trim off the extended triangles.

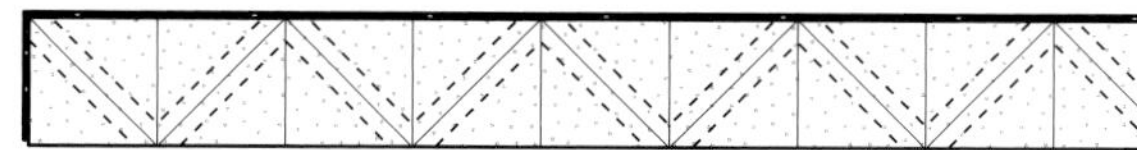

Mark 180 squares.

Make 360 triangle-square units.

2. With a soft-lead pencil and a see-through ruler, draw a diagonal line on the wrong side of each black 1⅞" square.
3. With right sides together, place a black 1⅞" square on each corner of a plaid 5¼" square as shown. Stitch on the diagonal lines. Trim ¼" from the stitching lines; press the triangles and the seam allowances toward the corners. Repeat to make a total of nine units.

Make 9.

4. Join two triangle-square units, one black 2" triangle, and one template A piece as shown. Press the seam allowances as indicated. Repeat to make a total of 36 units.

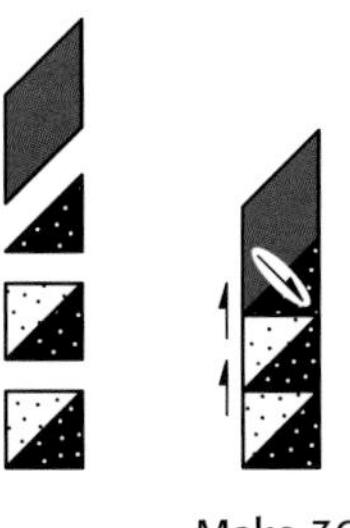

Make 36.

5. Join three triangle-square units, one black 2" triangle, and one template A piece as shown. Press the seam allowances as indicated. Repeat to make a total of 36 units.

Make 36.

6. Sew the steps 4 and 5 units to each white 5½" square as shown. Press the seam allowances toward the units. Make 36.

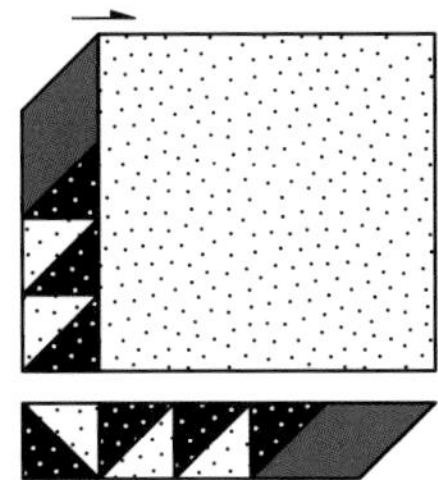

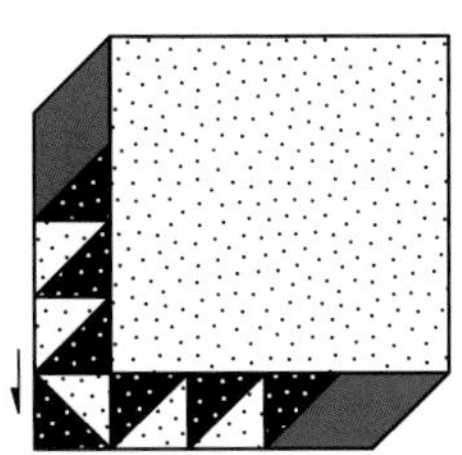

Make 36.

7. Join two triangle-square units and a black 2" triangle as shown. Press the seam allowances toward the triangle. Repeat to make a total of 36 units.

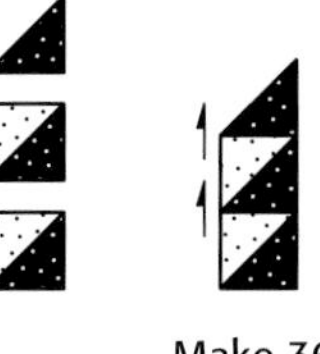

Make 36.

8. Join a black 2" triangle and three triangle-square units as shown. Press the seam allowances toward the triangle. Repeat to make a total of 36 units.

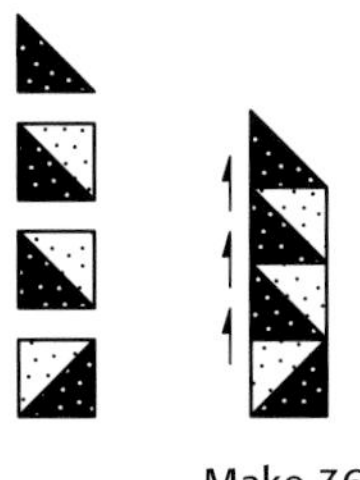

Make 36.

9. Sew the step 7 units to each white triangle as shown. Start stitching at the edge of the white triangle and stop stitching 1" from the point of the black triangle. Sew the step 8 units to the adjacent side of the white triangle as shown, again ending 1" from the black triangle. You'll complete these seams after the units are sewn to adjacent units. Repeat to make a total of 36 units.

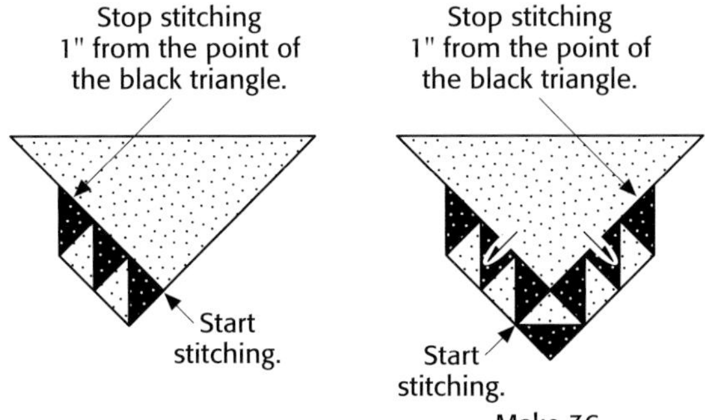

Make 36.

10. Sew a template B piece to the side of each step 9 unit as shown. Press the seam allowance toward the template B piece. Make 36.

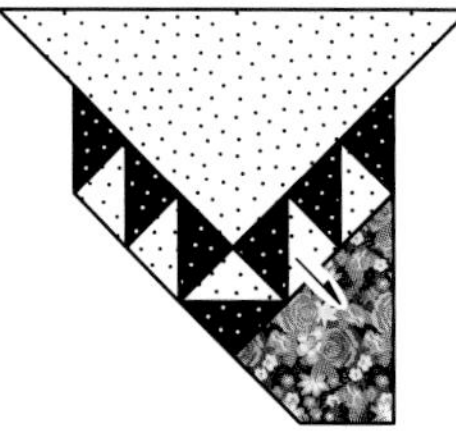

Make 36.

11. Sew a black 2¼" triangle to each of the remaining template B pieces as shown. Press the seam allowance toward the template B piece. Sew these units to the step 10 units. Press the seam allowances toward the template B pieces.

Make 36.

12. Arrange one step 3 unit, four step 6 units, and four step 11 units into three horizontal rows as shown.

13. Partially sew the units in each row together. Stitch from the straight edge to the diagonal edge as shown, stopping at the edge of the red diamonds and being careful not to catch the tips of the large white triangles in the seams. Press the seam allowance as indicated.

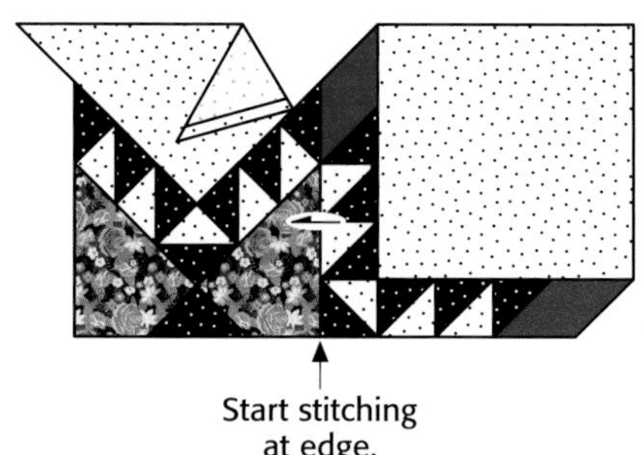

14. When all the units in the block are partially sewn together, go back and complete the seams, matching the raw edges, as shown.

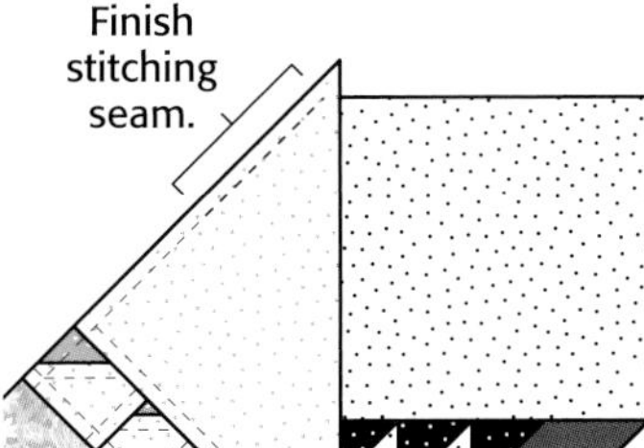

15. Sew the rows together to complete the block. Press the seam allowances as indicated.

16. Repeat steps 12–15 to make a total of nine blocks.

Make 9.

Assembling the Quilt Top

1. Sew four black-and-white floral 3¼" squares and three 3¼" x 17½" stripe pieces together as shown for the sashing. Press the seam allowances toward the sashing. Repeat to make a total of four sashing rows.

Make 4.

2. Sew together four 3¼" x 17½" stripe pieces and three blocks as shown. Press the seam allowances toward the sashing. Repeat to make a total of three block rows.

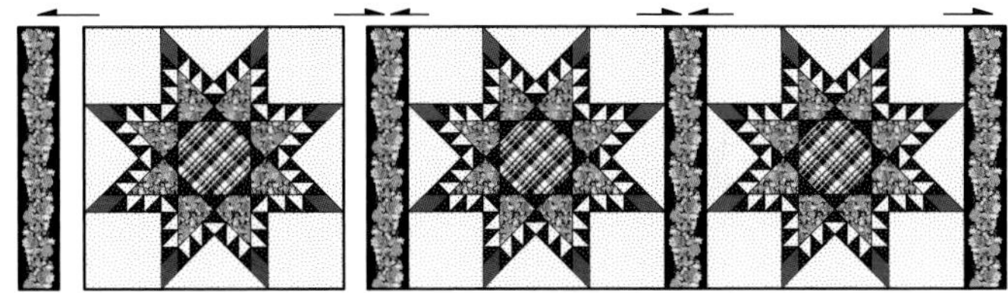

Make 3.

3. Arrange the sashing rows and the block rows as shown. Sew the rows together to complete the quilt center. Press the seam allowances in one direction.

4. Refer to "Straight-Cut Borders" on page 89 to add the plaid 4"-wide strips to the quilt for the border.

Finishing Your Quilt

Refer to "Quiltmaking Basics" on page 88 for specific instructions regarding each of the following steps.

1. Layer the quilt top with batting and backing; baste—unless you plan to take your quilt to a long-arm quilter.
2. Hand or machine quilt as desired.
3. Use the black 2¾"-wide strips to bind the quilt edges.
4. Embellish the quilt with the red buttons as shown in the photo on page 76.
5. Add a hanging sleeve to the back of the quilt if desired.

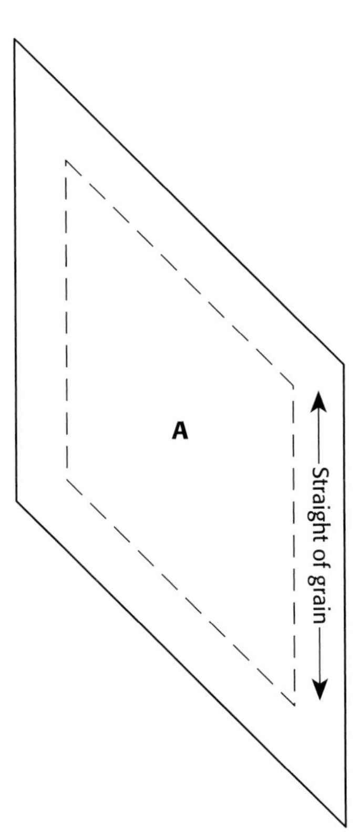
A
Straight of grain

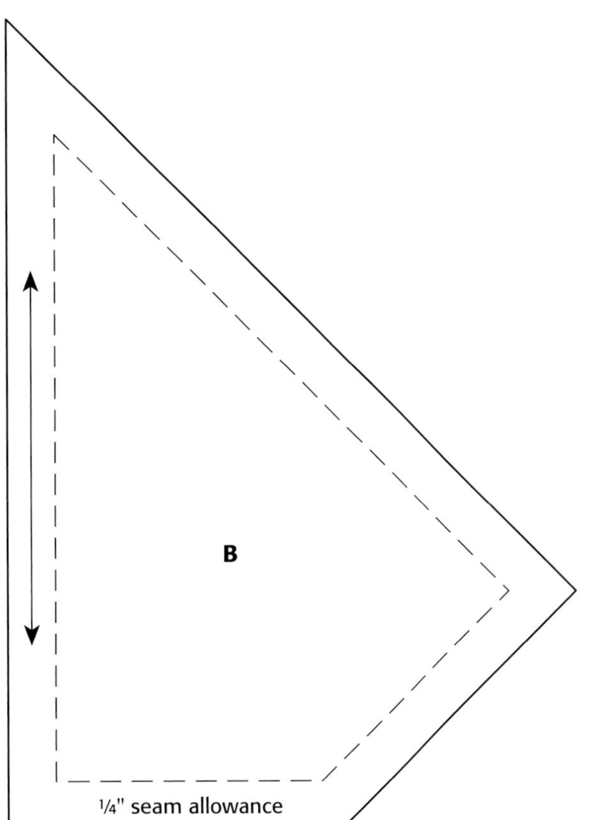
B
1/4" seam allowance

Hugs and Kisses

Skill level: *Beginner*

Finished quilt: 90½" x 102½" • **Finished blocks:** 6" x 6"

All the letters from our grandparents were signed "XOXOXO," and it always meant "hugs and kisses" to us. So XOXOXO to all of you! Wrap hugs and kisses around you with this quilt.
—Susan

Button Box

Because this is such a large quilt, the buttons are accents rather than the focus. I used a hodgepodge of red and maroon buttons to add colorful details. Remember that buttons don't have to match. In fact, a variety of shapes and colors adds more interest than a group of perfectly matching buttons.

Materials

Yardages are based on 42"-wide fabric.

4⅛ yards of cream print for blocks and squares
2¼ yards of red print for blocks and squares
2¼ yards of green print for blocks and squares
2 yards of maroon print for blocks and binding
8⅛ yards of fabric for backing
98" x 110" piece of batting
25 *total* red and maroon buttons, ¾" to 1" diameter

Cutting

All measurements include ¼"-wide seam allowances.

From the cream print, cut:

- 11 strips, 6½" x 42"; crosscut into 64 squares, 6½" x 6½"
- 12 strips, 3½" x 42"; crosscut into 128 squares, 3½" x 3½"
- 10 strips, 2½" x 42"

From the red print, cut:

- 11 strips, 6½" x 42"; crosscut into 64 squares, 6½" x 6½"

From the green print, cut:

- 11 strips, 6½" x 42"; crosscut into 63 squares, 6½" x 6½"

From the maroon print, cut:

- 8 strips, 2½" x 42"
- 10 strips, 1½" x 42"; crosscut into 256 squares, 1½" x 1½"
- 2 strips, 1¼" x 42"; crosscut into 64 squares, 1¼" x 1¼"
- 10 strips, 2¾" x 42"

Making the Blocks

1. To make the Nine Patch blocks, sew a cream 2½"-wide strip between two maroon 2½"-wide strips. Press the seam allowances toward the maroon. Make two strip sets. Crosscut the strip sets into 32 segments, 2½" wide.

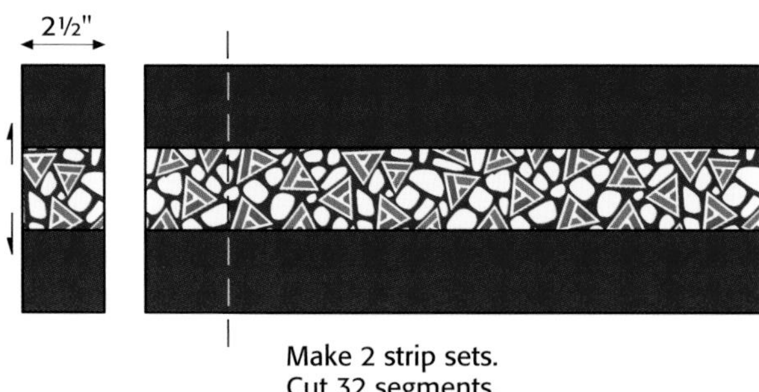

Make 2 strip sets.
Cut 32 segments.

2. Sew a maroon 2½"-wide strip between two cream 2½"-wide strips. Press the seam allowances toward the maroon. Make four strip sets. Crosscut the strip sets into 64 segments, 2½" wide.

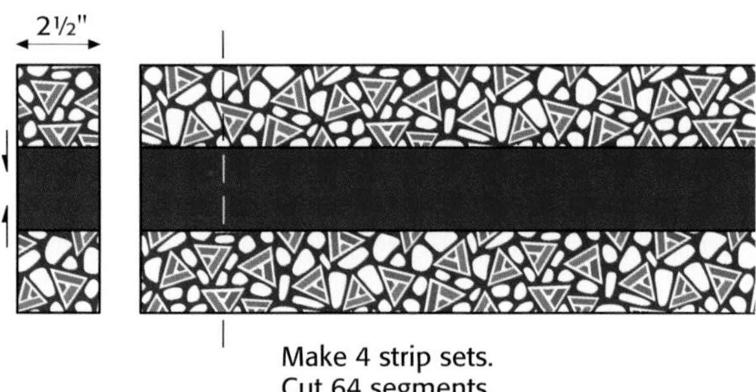

Make 4 strip sets.
Cut 64 segments.

3. Arrange one step 1 segment and two step 2 segments into three vertical rows as shown. Sew the rows together. Press the seam allowances toward the step 1 segment. Repeat to make a total of 32 blocks.

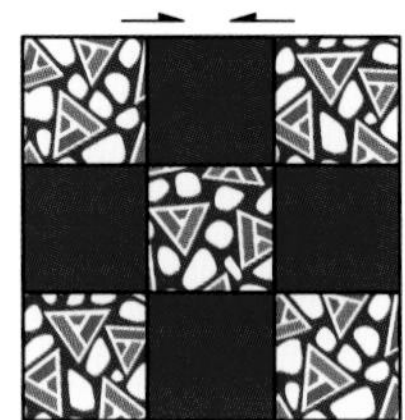

Make 32.

4. Using a soft-lead pencil and a see-through ruler, draw a diagonal line from corner to corner on the wrong side of each maroon 1½" and 1¼" square.

5. Position maroon 1½" squares on opposite corners of a cream 3½" square as shown. Stitch on the diagonal lines. Trim ¼" from the stitching lines; press the triangles and the seam allowances toward the corners.

Make 128.

6. To make the O blocks, arrange four step 5 units into two horizontal rows as shown. Stitch the units in each row together. Press the seam allowances in opposite directions. Sew the rows together. Press the seam allowance in one direction. Repeat to make a total of 16 blocks.

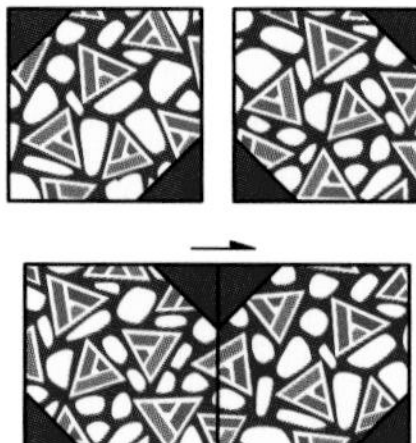
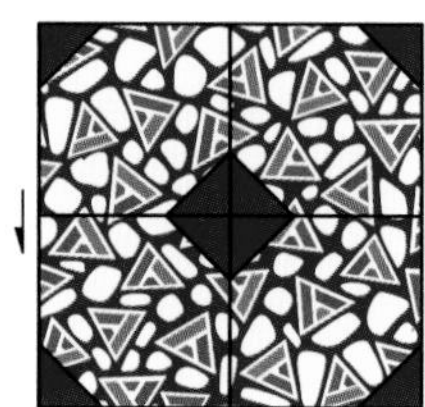

Make 16.

7. Position a maroon 1¼" square on one corner of each of the remaining step 5 units as shown. Stitch, trim, and press as before.

Make 64.

8. To make the X block, arrange four step 7 units into two horizontal rows as shown, positioning the units so the smaller triangles are in the outside corners. Sew the units in each row together. Press the seam allowances in opposite directions.

Sew the rows together. Press the seam allowance in one direction. Repeat to make a total of 16 blocks.

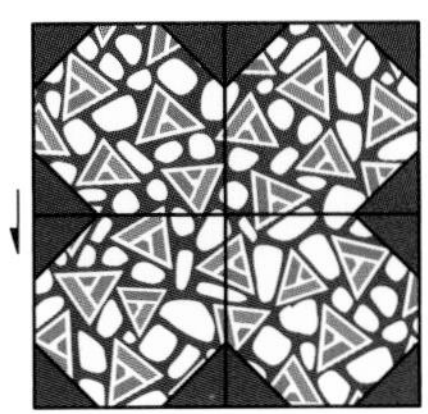

Make 16.

Assembling the Quilt Top

1. Arrange the blocks and 6½" squares into 17 horizontal rows as shown.
2. Stitch the pieces in each row together. Press all the seam allowances away from the cream squares and blocks. By consistently pressing like this, the seams will fit neatly together when joining the rows. Join the rows. Press the seam allowances in one direction.

Finishing Your Quilt

Refer to "Quiltmaking Basics" on page 88 for specific instructions regarding each of the following steps.

1. Layer the quilt top with batting and backing; baste—unless you plan to take your quilt to a long-arm quilter.
2. Hand or machine quilt as desired.
3. Use the maroon 2¾"-wide strips to bind the quilt edges.
4. Embellish the quilt with the buttons as shown in the photo on page 84, or create your own arrangement.

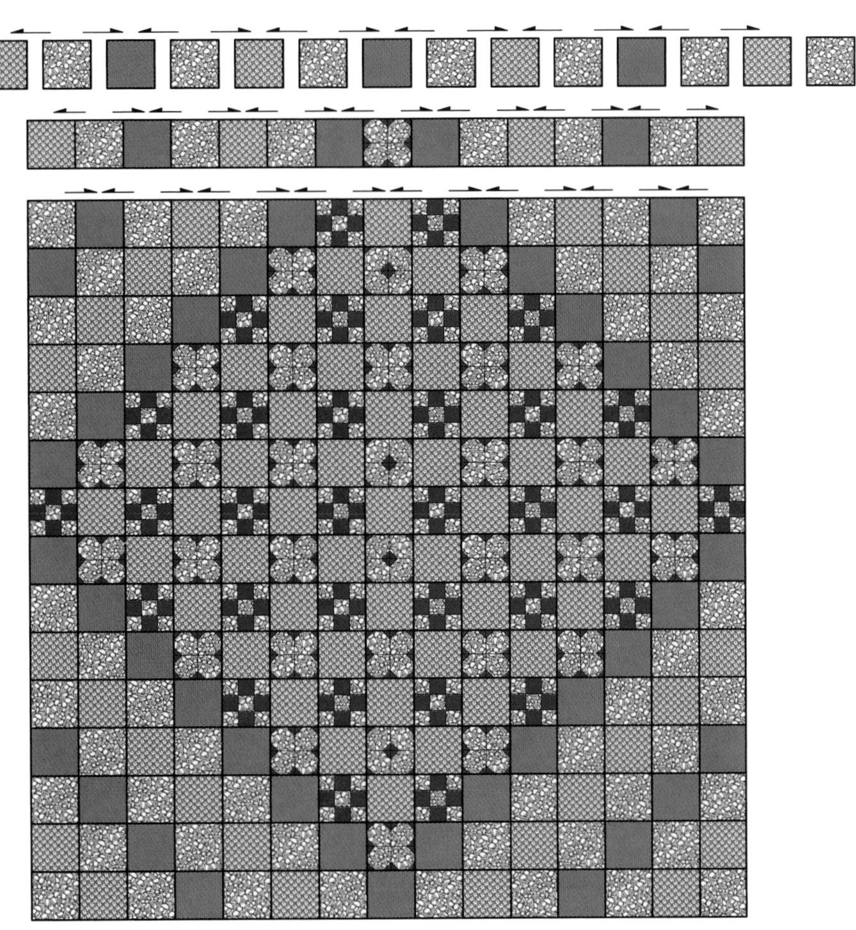

Quiltmaking Basics

This chapter offers helpful information for successfully completing the projects in this book. We're sharing techniques that we use in our quiltmaking, but you may prefer to use other methods. Accurate cutting, consistent seaming, and diligent pressing are important to keep in mind, but just relax and enjoy the process!

Selecting and Preparing Fabric

Fabric quality is a key ingredient to a quality finished quilt, so pay attention to the fabric you're using in your quilt project and don't skimp. We recommend that you prewash fabrics to ensure that the colors won't bleed when your quilt is laundered the first time. We've both experienced the disaster of colors bleeding in a completed project, and we assure you that it's better to be safe than sorry.

Cutting

With the exception of appliqué motifs, all of the pieces for the projects in this book are cut with a rotary cutter. Always take great care when rotary cutting. Measure and cut your pieces accurately and be careful that you don't cut yourself. Get out a sharp, new rotary blade at the first sign of difficulty in making clean fabric cuts.

Cut out appliqué templates and fabric shapes with scissors to ensure accuracy. Use a different pair of scissors for cutting the paper or template-plastic shapes than you do for cutting the fabric shapes. Be sure the scissors you use for cutting fabric are sharp and be careful that you don't cut yourself.

Piecing

For successful piecing, use an exact ¼" seam allowance. Any variation in the seam allowance will affect the size of the block, which will in turn affect the size of other elements, such as sashing and borders.

It is well worth the money to invest in a ¼" foot for your particular machine. If a ¼" foot isn't available for your machine, create a seam guide by placing the ¼" mark of an acrylic ruler under the needle. Place the edge of a piece of tape or moleskin along the edge of the ruler.

Pressing

Take the time to press your fabric after each step, following the directional arrows in the diagrams. Try using a thick terry towel on your ironing board for the pressing surface. It allows the steam to penetrate the fabric for crisp pressing.

Appliquéing with Fusible Web

There are several methods for appliquéing. For the quilts in this book, we chose to use fusible appliqué. We find it to be fast, easy, and attractive. You cut the fabric shapes without adding a turn-under seam allowance and then simply fuse them to the background. You can stitch around the appliqué edges to make the quilt durable for washing, or you can leave the edges exposed for a quick, easy project.

1. Trace each individual appliqué pattern onto the paper side of the paper-backed fusible web. If the pattern is asymmetrical, *it must be reversed.* Group

all of the pieces that will be cut from the same fabric, leaving about ¼" between them. Cut around each individual shape or the entire group of appliqué shapes if they will be cut from the same fabric, leaving about a ⅛" margin.

2. Place the shape or group of shapes on the wrong side of the appropriate fabric, paper side up. Follow the manufacturer's instructions to fuse the shapes in place.
3. Carefully cut out the appliqué pieces on the traced lines and peel away the paper backing. Arrange the fabric shapes, right side up, on the block background and fuse into place, following the manufacturer's instructions.
4. If you want to stitch the appliqués in place to further secure them or add decorative detailing, attach an open-toe appliqué foot to your machine. This will allow you to see the needle clearly. Thread your machine with a lightweight (60-weight) embroidery thread that matches the appliqué.
5. Set your machine for the desired stitch. Use a satin stitch, blanket stitch, or feather stitch to stitch completely around the appliqué shapes.

Adding Borders

Generally speaking, the most stable borders are cut from the lengthwise grain of the fabric rather than from the crosswise grain, but because lengthwise-grain borders require more fabric, most patterns are written to use the crosswise grain. You have to decide what is the most valuable to you: economy of fabric or maximum flatness of your quilt.

For the projects in this book, the yardage requirements reflect crosswise-cut strips. Cut strips as indicated in the cutting instructions for your quilt. If the quilt is larger than the length of one strip, you'll need to sew the strips together end to end, and then cut strips the exact length from the longer strip.

Straight-Cut Borders

1. Measure the quilt through the vertical center and cut two border strips to this measurement, joining strips as necessary.
2. Pin-mark the centers of the quilt edges and the border strips. Pin the border strips to the quilt sides, matching the center marks and ends. Sew the border strips to the quilt, easing as necessary, and press the seam allowances toward the border strips.

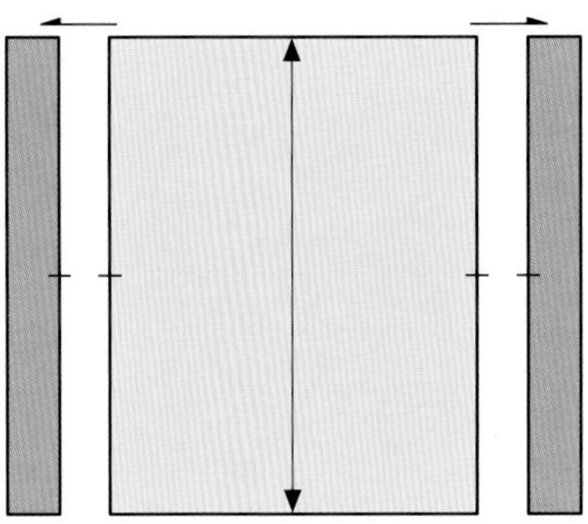

Measure the center of the quilt, top to bottom. Mark the centers.

3. Measure your quilt through the horizontal center and cut two border strips to this measurement, joining strips as necessary. Again, mark the centers of the quilt edges and the border strips. Pin the border strips to the top and bottom edges of the quilt, matching the center marks and ends. Sew the border strips to the quilt, easing as necessary, and press the seam allowances toward the newly added border strips.

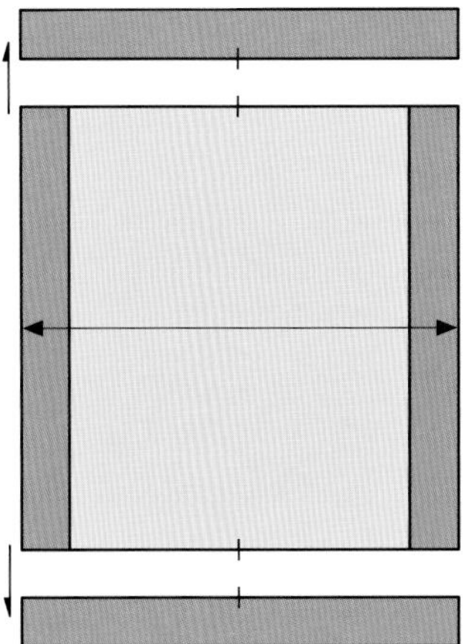

Measure the center of the quilt, side to side, including the borders. Mark the centers.

Mitered Borders

Strips for a mitered border are cut extra long and trimmed to fit after stitching the mitered corners.

1. Measure each edge of the quilt. For each edge, cut a strip the length measured plus twice the border width plus an extra 5". Place a pin at each end of the side borders to mark the length of the quilt top. Place a pin at each end of the top and bottom borders to mark the width of the quilt top.

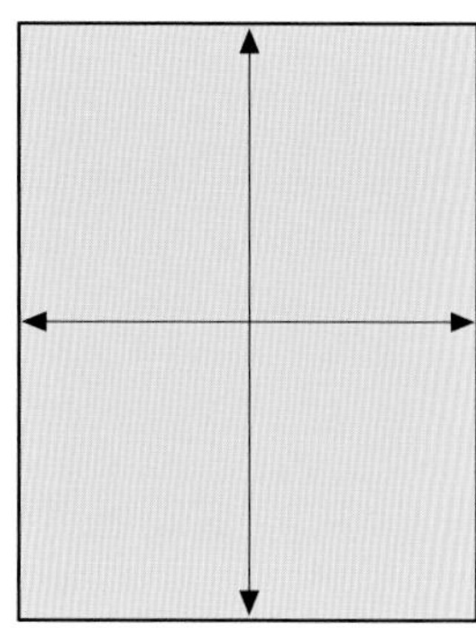

2. Pin-mark the centers of the quilt edges and the border strips. Pin-mark ¼" from each corner on the quilt top.
3. Pin the top border strip to the top edge of the quilt, matching the center points and aligning the pins at the ends of the border strip with the ¼" marks on the quilt. An even amount of excess border strip should extend beyond the quilt-top edges. Stitch, beginning and ending the seam ¼" from the quilt-top corners. Repeat with the remaining border strips.

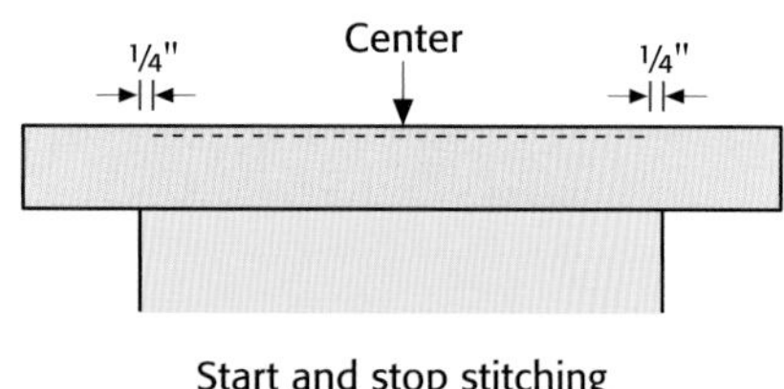

Start and stop stitching ¼" from the quilt edge.

4. Working on a flat surface, place one border on top of the other at a 90° angle.

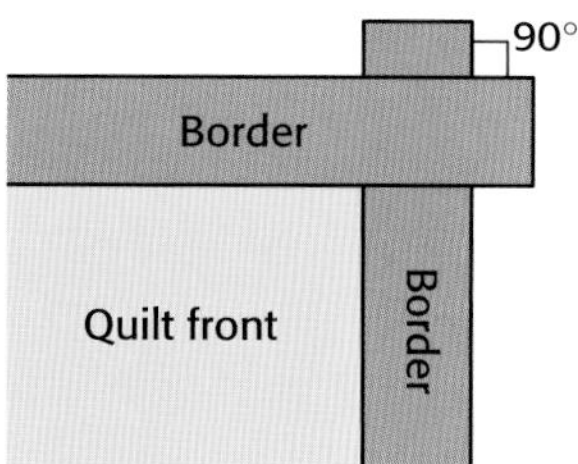

5. Fold the top-border layer back at a 45° angle and press to mark the stitching line.

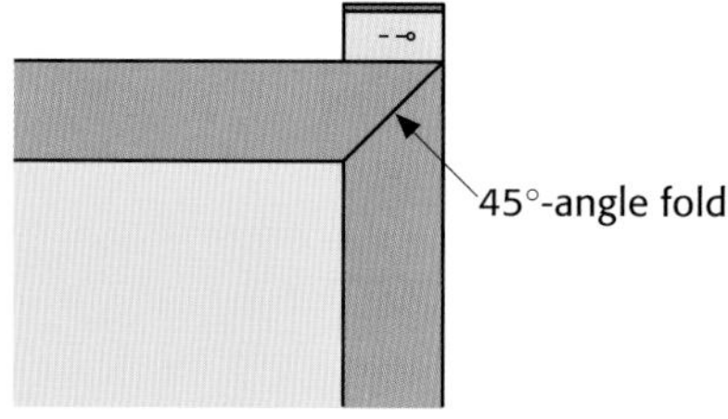

6. With right sides together, pin the border strips together. Begin stitching ¼" from the inner corner and sew on the crease line. Backstitch as you begin and end the stitching.

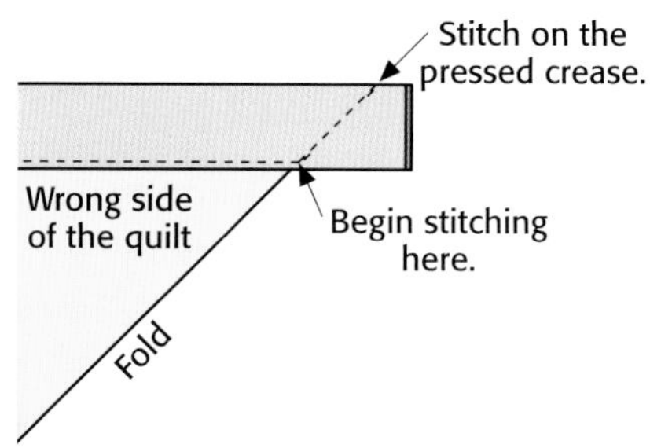

7. Trim away the excess border fabric, leaving a ¼"-wide seam allowance. Press the seam open. Repeat with the remaining corners.

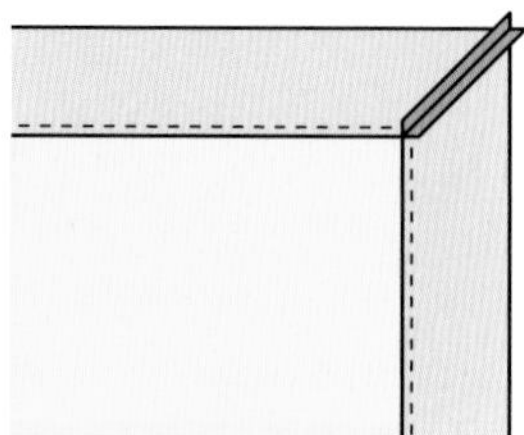

Trim the mitered seams and press open.

Preparing the Backing

Because the selvages are more tightly woven than the rest of the fabric, always trim away the selvages when preparing your backing. This will keep the seams from puckering. Cut the backing fabric 4" to 8" larger than the quilt top, regardless of how you plan to quilt it (hand, long-arm or domestic machine quilting, or tying). The larger the top, the more generous the backing allowance should be.

Depending on the size of the quilt, it may be necessary to piece the backing by sewing two or three lengths of fabric together to achieve the needed size. The seams can run vertically or horizontally. Use a ½" seam allowance to piece the backing. Press the seams open to reduce bulk for the quilting process.

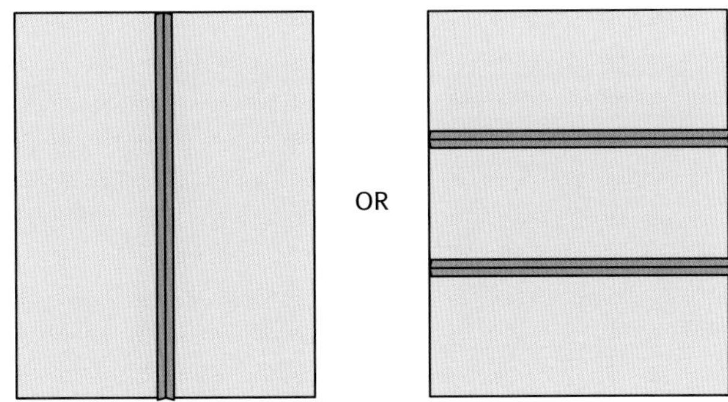

Taking Your Quilt to a Long-Arm Machine Quilter

You may want to have your quilt quilted by a long-arm machine quilter. Check with your local quilt shop or guild for a recommended long-arm quilter in your area. Usually, the machine quilter has the batting and the thread available for you, but a phone call to the quilter can clarify exactly what you need to bring. Have your top and backing fabric well pressed, and trim away all stray threads so that it is ready for quilting. It is a good idea to fold your top and backing neatly and hang it on a hanger to take to the quilter. Don't layer your quilt for the long-arm quilter.

Assembling the Layers

If you aren't taking your quilt to a long-arm machine quilter, the next step is to layer the quilt top, batting, and backing.

1. Spread out the pressed backing on a flat, clean surface, wrong side up. Secure the edges with masking tape, being careful not to stretch the backing out of shape.
2. Center the batting over the backing, smoothing out any wrinkles.
3. Center the pressed quilt top, right side up, on the batting, smoothing out any wrinkles and keeping the quilt edges parallel to the backing edges.
4. Baste the layers together with hand stitching if you plan on hand quilting, or use size 1 rustproof safety pins if you're machine quilting.

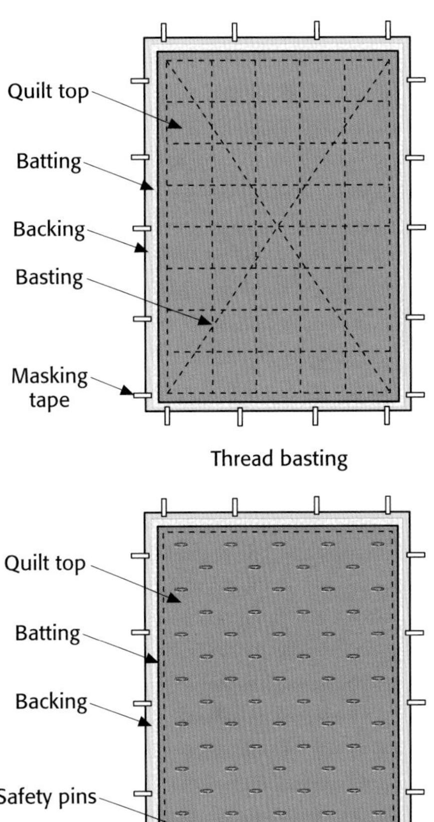

Quilting

The next step is to permanently secure the layers together. It is a personal choice as to whether you want to hand or machine quilt your projects. There are many excellent books available to guide you through either process.

When the quilting is complete, leave the basting stitches around the edges intact and remove the remaining basting stitches or any pins that weren't removed while quilting. Trim the batting and backing even with the quilt top and make sure the corners are square.

Binding Your Quilt

Using a French double-fold binding gives a durable finish to your quilt, and the strips can easily be cut across the width of the fabric. This type of binding is referred to as "straight-cut" binding. It is adequate for quilts with straight edges and 90° corners. The finished width of the binding depends on the width of the strips cut. The patterns in this book use binding strips that are cut 2¾" wide and create a finished binding of just under ½". If you prefer a narrower binding, cut your strips accordingly.

1. Join the strips end to end to make one continuous strip. Trim the seam allowances to ¼" and press them open.
2. Trim one end of the binding strip at a 45° angle. Press under the trimmed end ¼". This will be your starting end. Press the strip in half lengthwise, wrong sides together.

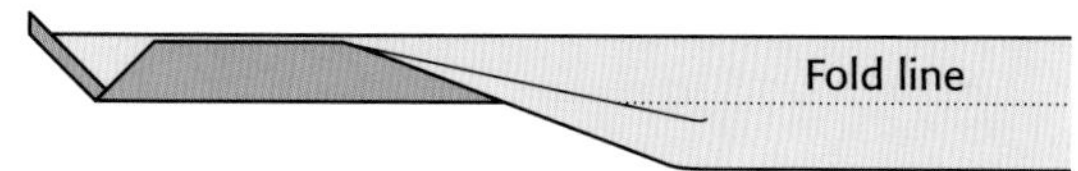

3. Pick a beginning point on your quilt edge, away from a corner. Align the raw edges of the binding with the raw edges of the quilt. Leaving the first 3" of the binding unstitched, stitch the binding in place, using a walking foot and a generous ¼" seam allowance. Stop stitching ¼" from the corner, backstitch, and remove the quilt from the machine.

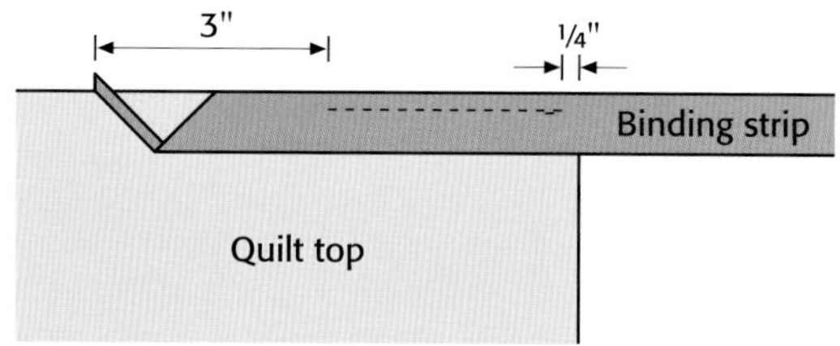

4. Turn the quilt a quarter turn so you're ready to stitch the next edge. Fold the binding straight up, forming a 45° angle. Then bring the binding straight down, aligning the edge of the binding with the edge of the quilt, and the newly formed fold of binding with the top edge of the quilt. Start stitching at the top edge and sew though all layers, stopping ¼" from the next corner. Repeat the process at each corner around the quilt.

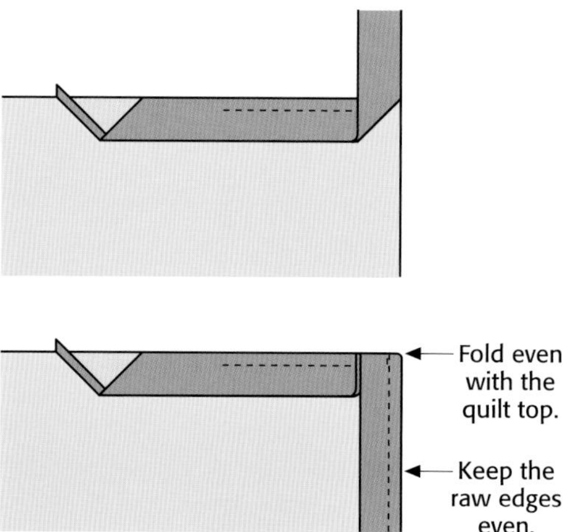

5. When you reach the point where you began, tuck the end into the starting end and trim away the excess. Continue sewing the binding to the quilt.

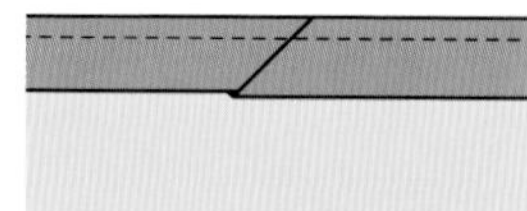

6. Fold the binding over the raw edges of the quilt to the back so that the fold of the binding covers the machine stitching. Hand stitch the binding in place, mitering the corners so the miter folds in the opposite direction from the fold on the quilt front.

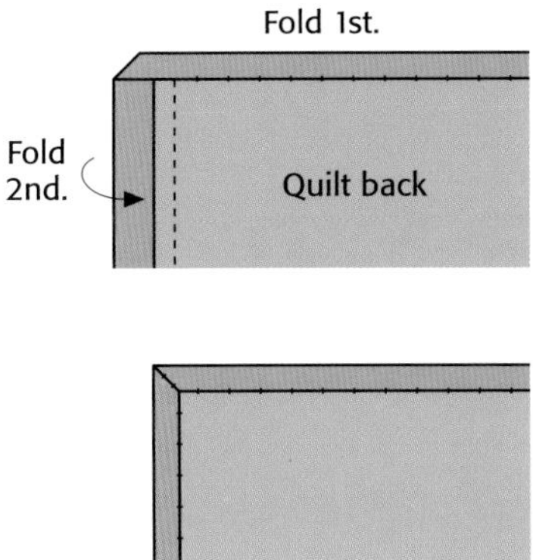

Adding a Hanging Sleeve

Quilts that are hung for display may require a hanging sleeve on the back. A dowel or curtain rod slipped through the sleeve can hang from wall brackets.

1. Cut a 6"-wide fabric piece that measures the length of the quilt, plus 2". Turn under a ¼" hem on both ends and press; then turn under 1" more. Press and topstitch each end.
2. Fold the strip in half lengthwise, wrong sides together. Using a ½" seam allowance, sew the long raw edges together. Press the seam allowance open, centering the seam on the side of the tube. With the seam facing the back of the quilt, center the tube just below the quilt binding at the top of the quilt.
3. Slipstitch the top and bottom edges of the sleeve to the quilt backing, making sure that no stitches go through to the front of the quilt.

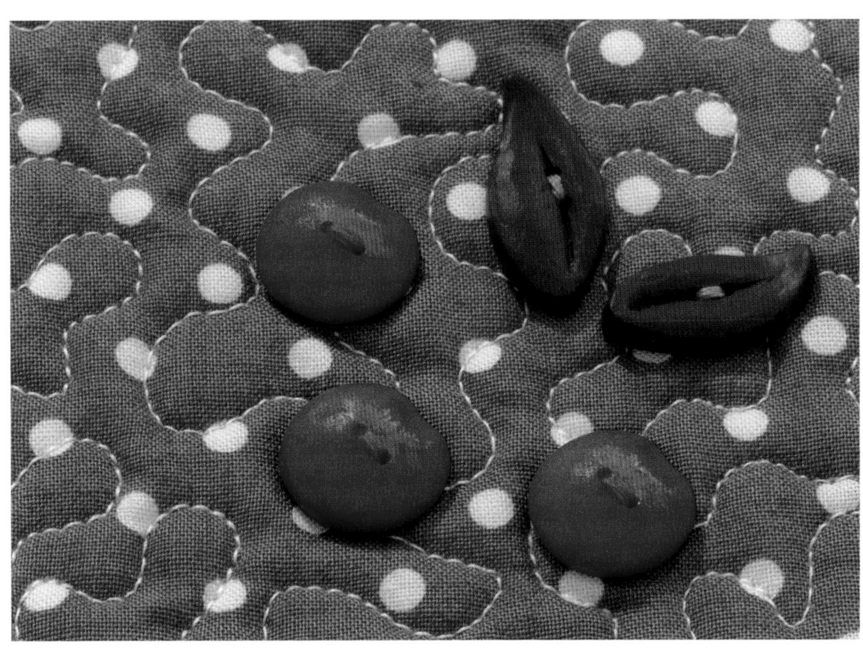

About the Authors

Loraine Manwaring

Loraine Manwaring and Susan Nelsen are sisters who both enjoy quilting. Loraine started sewing at the age of eight when she received a small Singer sewing machine as a gift. Her grandmother helped her sew a dress for herself on the tiny chain-stitch machine, and she has loved sewing ever since. When her children were young, she began teaching basic sewing to a women's group at church, and this led to teaching beginning quilting classes as well. She has taught various fabric arts ever since and has been designing her own patterns and quilting projects for years. She is appreciative of her grandmother and the many accomplished-quilter friends, who have taught her over the years. She holds a degree in elementary education from Utah State University. Loraine and her husband, Mark, raised their family in Washington and currently live in Utah at the foot of the rugged Wasatch Mountains. They are the parents of five grown children. Loraine enjoys creating new quilt designs, traveling the world, and spending time with her grandchildren.

Susan Nelsen

Susan loves the creative experience of working with fabrics and colors and has been quilting for what seems like forever. She thrives on designing and is the owner of Rasmatazz Designs, an original quilt-pattern company and a long-arm machine-quilting business. She can be found at her computer, her sewing machine, or her long-arm machine anytime, day or night. Along with 20 patterns, she has published one other book.

She has a degree in elementary education from Utah State University and worked as a substitute teacher while her children were growing up. She worked for several years at a local quilt shop and continues to teach machine quilting for home sewing machines. In addition, she enjoys working as a freelance editor for quilting books and projects.

After traversing the country for more than twenty-five years with the United States Air Force, Susan and her husband, Ken, moved to Idaho Falls, Idaho, following Ken's retirement seven years ago. They have three terrific sons and a talented daughter. They thoroughly enjoy the role of grandparents to their grandchildren.